The Joy of Wildlife Gardening – an RSPB Guide

by Geoffrey Smith

The Joy of Wildlife Gardening – an RSPB Guide

by Geoffrey Smith

Published by The Royal Society for the Protection of Birds,
The Lodge, Sandy, Bedfordshire SG19 2DL.

ISBN No 0 903138 31 X

Designed by Patsy Hinchliffe
Illustrations by Jane Leycester Paige
Line drawings by Darren Rees
Typesetting by Bedford Typesetters Ltd
Origination by Saxon Photolitho Ltd
Printing and binding by W. S. Cowell Ltd
Distribution by Christopher Helm (Publishers) Ltd

Contents

The Joy of Wildlife Gardening

Introduction

All of us must at some time in our lives have been aware of the glorious loveliness of unspoiled countryside. Beauty of morning in a copse alive with bird song, the cuckoo calling over a valley shimmering in the warmth of a June day. To stand on a Norfolk breckland being rained on by lark song, or take the sharp winds of spring close to the moor edge with the curlew's call for company is to enjoy a brief communion with short-lived gladsome things.

Equally, those who take pleasure in the moors, fields, and woods, who find respite in company with the wildlife which abounds there, must also be aware of the speed at which the remaining wilderness areas are being lost. With growing awareness of the often wanton despoliation comes a sense of impotence, a powerlessness to halt the decline except to shout 'wealth pursued is no guarantee of happiness'.

In fact, there is something that everyone with access to a garden can do, for gardens are as much a part of the countryside as the rivers, fields, woods, and moors of the landscape beyond. Linked together they form bands of habitat down which can flow a busy traffic of wildlife. In creating a garden which serves as a posting house to some, a permanent residence for others, and hunting ground to a few, there is opportunity to share in that world of nature, so finely balanced that even our widow's mite of green earth could make the difference between survival and extinction.

A garden can be contrived to combine the twin functions of wildlife conservation and personal pleasure, yet still be beautiful to look at. Indeed, it would appear to me that the two are in themselves complementary. In our efforts to attract the widest possible range of birds, insects, mammals and other itinerants to share garden space with us, some of the therapeutic benefits become immediately apparent. The observation of wildlife has been for me since early childhood a remedy against, and antidote to, the pressures of modern living.

Transferring a basic understanding of even the rudimentary aspects of conservation, to give them practical relevance in the garden, can become an absorbing pastime. Some knowledge of plants is essential which adds yet another facet to the study. Such information, elementary though it may be, enables the novice conservationist to achieve the type of garden which will be our own important bulwark in defence of conservation, and bring relief from the sense of impotence at being unable to do anything to preserve our native flora and fauna.

1. The countryside in your garden

Gardens are well cultivated not as they are fertile but as they are safe for all to share

A garden is for me a place which captures something of the beauty and delight that I find in the open countryside. Green leaves, pattern of flowers, and the busy life they attract to them, make an ever changing tableau which fashions a deep, abiding silence of growing things.

Thirty years ago I never thought of my garden as anything other than a piece of earth on which to grow flowers, fruit, and vegetables: a cornucopia on a grand scale. Gradually the awareness dawned that my own garden and others like it were being increasingly recognised for the contribution they can make as refuges and feeding 'stations' for wildlife.

Increasingly the established patterns of agriculture were changing, so that the seasonal rhythms and cropping methods no longer fitted smoothly into a natural ecological system. For example, even the farms normally restricted by their height above sea level and quality of their soil to just one hay crop a year, can now, by liberal use of fertilizer and modern machinery, take two crops of silage. The havoc this causes to ground-nesting birds is a tragedy further compounded by the practice of slurry spreading on a year-round basis. Yet no-one expects farmers to work the land by old-fashioned, labour intensive, traditional methods; they have a living to make in the most economical way that modern technology permits.

The influence any of us can bring to bear on how the now limited tracts of countryside are preserved as living entities, rather than museums, is at best collective rather than individual. Within the boundaries of our own gardens we can exercise near complete control. That my own garden and others like it are more than just plots of ground in which to indulge an interest in plant cultivation, is now obvious. Gardens have taken on a new importance, for together they form green corridors linking the ever-decreasing wilderness areas together. A nettle-filled, overgrown copse, in a vast expanse of brick and concrete might just survive as an isolated island, a haven for wildlife though in a limited, inert form. By providing a green highway of gardens to link one of the wilderness habitats to another, we permit an intercourse between the two. As a result, each is less fragmented and vulnerable, and both are more easily able to change and adapt.

Conservation is not, as we sometimes delude ourselves into believing, a new concept, for it is practised now and has been for thousands of years by primitive man. A tribe moves into an area then exploits the endemic resources of flora and fauna to the full before moving on. The natural resources were rarely depleted to the point where they could

9

not recover, nor did they suffer further exploitation until the ecological balance was completely restored. Over recent years the depletion of the world's natural assets has accelerated, almost as if the resources at our disposal were inexhaustible.

The landowning aristocracy were in many senses custodians of natural resources. There was, for the space of several hundred years, faith in the future, in that the traditional system would continue. There would be time for the woodlands of oak, ash, beech, and maple to mature as a source of pleasure or income to generations as yet unborn. That the grove of walnut planted by one generation might take a quarter of a century to produce fruit was never considered important. Walnuts there had always been, so the continuity of young, vigorous, heavy cropping trees should endure. There was a concern for the well being of the soil that was not totally engendered by self interest. Good husbandry was both instinctive and traditional: the rule to always put in a little more than is taken out was then generally accepted. All this has changed in a progression accelerated by two wars, when mere survival took precedence over all else. Woodlands were felled and either not replaced, or any replanting done was with quick maturing softwoods. Centuries old hedges were ripped out to make way for ever increasing mechanisation. The soil was persuaded to respond to a monoculture system of farming. Any of the deficiencies resulting from the one crop system, as opposed to the old three or four course rotation, are easily corrected by a dressing of fertilizer. Build-up of pests or diseases can be controlled by a whole armoury of chemical sprays. Weeds of cultivation are no longer a factor to be considered when a tank full of selective weed control will leave the crop free from competition.

So, inevitably, it seems the destruction of habitat must continue even though a land populated by man and his domestic animals is little more than a clinical, sterile desert. Just before impotence gives way to despair, like finding a spring of crystal-clear water in the desert, comes the assurance that a garden can be formed into a most effective conservation area. Within the boundaries of our domain, weeds can be push-hoed, not killed off with selective killers. Caterpillars on the cabbages are a food source for nestlings: those the birds miss can be hand-picked. Shrubs which offer for our enjoyment flowers, fruit, foliage, or coloured stems, function admirably as nesting sites. The insects which are attracted by flowers are at one and the same time a food source themselves, and providers against winter famine in the form of ripe fruit which develops from pollinated flowers.

That every conscious effort we make to attract and encourage the birds, butterflies, insects, and other animals into our gardens will be repaid in abundance by the pleasure we will derive from watching them quickly becomes apparent. Combine this with a sense of satisfaction that instead of being just an impotent bystander, aware of, but unable to halt the destruction of our remaining unspoiled countryside, we can in our own gardens provide a place of respite for our beleaguered flora and fauna. That we shall benefit in the process from a closer communion with the abiding things is of incalculable value in terms of personal well being.

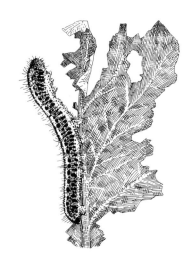

Caterpillars of several butterflies, including large and small whites, feed on the leaves of cabbages and other brassicas. They in turn provide food for birds and the gardener can easily hand-pick them off affected plants rather than resorting to pesticides.

A wildlife garden is in practical terms a place which provides attractive surroundings for us, while offering access and hospitality to as many birds, reptiles, insects, animals and others that the area at our disposal can support. What never fails to surprise me is the speed at which birds and animals adapt to new surroundings. I am also elated and encouraged by the way my presence is accepted as a peaceable part of the whole.

The first priority is to plant shrubs, and where possible trees, which in due course will grow to give shelter from predators and the weather. That they will in themselves become a food source is also important. This initial planting is the first link in the chain where each individual unit is so totally interdependent that if one part is destroyed then all that remain are threatened. An example would be *Cotoneaster* × 'Hybridus Pendulus' one of my top priority plantings when designing a garden. The flowers are attractive to insects, birds feed on the insects that pollinate the flowers which in due course turn into berries for a different species of bird to feed on during the winter. Where the branches touch the soil they grow into a dense carpet which even in dry weather ensures the soil stays moist, so forming a suitable breeding ground for slugs, worms, and other lovers of close, humid, cool conditions. Hedgehogs, voles, blackbirds, and the like soon discover such a well stocked larder, so yet another link is forged in a chain which began with one shrub. Last year a dunnock built a nest in the tangled head of branches and raised three nestlings to maturity, so the dependence grows. Remove the *Cotoneaster* and the whole, closely interdependent structure collapses.

Let me here point out that the life of a garden is never static. There are some permanent residents, otherwise the pattern is fluid. Seasonal changes, hibernation, migration, and population decline or explosion are a part of a complex ecology. Herbaceous plants, multi-flowered annuals, and bulbs will cater for the busy concourse of life which centres on the garden during summer. Some of this, what I call the plant sub-strata, will be selected because they are food source for bees, moths, butterflies, and a whole concourse of insects. Others, like nasturtiums or sunflowers, play a dual role first to the insects when the flowers open, then to greenfinches and other birds as the seeds ripen.

We the gardeners become a part of the seasonal rhythm, and to do this we must be aware of the movement and exchange which goes on between the garden and the world outside. Almost as the swallows leave so fieldfares, redwings, and other winter visitors move in to strip the berries from holly and hawthorn in the hedgerows and ornamental shrubs in the garden. Being aware of this trafficking, every effort is made to supplement food supplies, nesting sites, and other amenities as necessary without interfering more than need be with the natural order of things. The peanut dispensers, mixed seeds, meal worms, household scraps or chopped suet are in these terms a supplement, not meddling. There is a reward for the provider of such avian gastronomic delights in the ever changing, fascinating, sometimes dramatic theatre of wildlife brought within view of a conveniently situated window.

Making available additional secure nesting sites or bat roosts with

Dunnock gathering nest material. Shrubs and trees are valuable for birds: providing food, shelter, song posts and nest sites.

Harry Smith Horticultural Collection

Ox-eye daisies mix with thistles, poppies and plantains in wild profusion.

strategically placed boxes is yet another means of improving the existing facilities without interrupting or rendering artificial, except in a minor degree, the pattern of life which evolves in the garden environment.

The restrictions imposed by limited space are obvious and perforce have to be accepted. Yet in the garden as elsewhere the laws of natural selection apply; the fittest, most adaptable survive as they do in the woods and fields beyond the garden boundaries. In this it is not wise to intervene. Magpies and crows make free of the food I put out, and there is a temptation to frighten them away in favour of what I might consider to be more attractive species. Apart from the fact that my intrusion would scare all the other birds out of the garden at the same time, making myself a judge of which species shall be allowed access defeats the object, which was to provide as natural a habitat as possible within the limits imposed by lack of space. The young sparrowhawk who found the garden a profitable hunting ground discovered, after the first element of surprise had worn off, that the survivors soon learnt to defeat his purpose. The pattern of survival established through centuries still applies; either adapt to changing circumstances or die.

There is one hazard evident, and certainly more lethal, which the wild creatures adjusting to a garden habitat may encounter, and that is the cat – feral or domestic. There are ways to mitigate the threat presented by your own or a neighbour's cat. Always place the bird-table well away from any sort of cover that would enable a cat to stalk feeding birds. Even though the birds feeding on the table may be out of pouncing range, some, the dunnock for example, feed like Lazarus on the crumbs which drop onto the soil below, and they are then vulnerable. Nesting-boxes need to be placed out of reach, remembering that cats, or at least some of them, are excellent climbers.

To turn a cat into a modern version of the mediaeval leper by hanging a bell around the unfortunate animal's neck warns the birds of danger. I once had the task of rescuing a cat that was being slowly asphyxiated as it hung from a branch stub which had caught behind the bell festooned collar. In my experience, cats are not compatible with wildlife gardens.

All the suggestions so far have been concerned with individual effort, which when combined with those of our neighbours, spreads like the ripples in a pool, becoming a major contribution to wildlife conservation. This collectivism is even more of a potent force when joined to one or other of the bodies concerned with husbanding our natural resources, and defending them against exploitation. There is a list of conservation organisations on page 156 at the back of this book. Some are specialist, concentrating their efforts on conserving one vulnerable species, for example the British Hedgehog Preservation Society. Others, like The Royal Society for Protection of Birds (RSPB) and the Royal Society for Nature Conservation (RSNC), are involved with the broader aspects of conserving the unique flora and fauna which shares this country's limited resources. Each and every one deserves the unqualified support of all those who are seeking to prevent further despoliation of the natural world around us.

2. A personal Eden

The garden habitat

A fine male brambling, a winter visitor to Great Britain from Scandinavia, comes to drink at a small pond.

There is a vast difference between the garden we would like to eventually achieve and the reality which the limits of circumstance force upon us. The dream assumes an ideal site, reality persuades us to accept a situation which is far from perfect. I have a vision of a personal Eden so clear in detail that the place must exist outside my imagination. A woodland of mature beech, oak and holly, fringed with dog rose, hawthorn, hazel, and rowan forms the northern boundary. At the bottom of a field which slopes gently away from the house there is a spring-fed stream. What is remarkable is that the soil is quite obviously alkaline, and for someone who enjoys growing lime intolerant plants that shows an extraordinary deviation from type.

Reality is a little over half an acre (0·25 ha) of light acid loam on an exposed hillside. The trees growing in the borders are for the most part those I planted 11 years ago. There is a pool because I dug the hole by the sweat of my brow to make it. Last winter I recorded 27 different species of birds feeding on the lawn and compost bin lid which also functions as a table where I scatter corn, seeds, and other delicacies. I also have access to a copse just the width of a lane away, fringed with an unkempt hedge of snowberry, hawthorn, sycamore, birdcherry, ash, and holly. The remaining space, approximately a third of an acre (0·14 ha) is six feet (1·83 m) high in nettles, although I cut about half of these down in late May to give tortoiseshell butterflies succulent young shoots on which to lay their eggs. There are docks and dandelions along the wide lane verges bordering the garden, so all I am doing with my delving and planting is to further enrich the basic habitat which exists here already.

From my own experience I would question whether the unkempt wilderness of nettles, elderberry, and willowherb in the copse is of more value in conservation terms than the garden. For a few specialist species the copse is a most essential part of a chain providing food in the shape of nettles for the caterpillars to feed on. The bird which takes the caterpillar to nestlings is less dependent for there are equally acceptable and nutritious food sources available elsewhere. In some areas, the natural food your garden has to offer can play an important part, especially in winter.

Nettles are essential breeding sites for several very handsome native butterflies including red admiral, peacock, and small tortoise-shell, so had the copse not filled the need so admirably I would have allowed a clump of nettles to spring up around the compost heap. The tops do make excellent compost if cut early – as they need to be in late May, so once again the requirements of garden and butterfly are both

15

The Joy of Wildlife Gardening

served. Watching peacock, tortoiseshell, and red admiral butterflies feeding on *Buddleia*, and Michaelmas daisy in September assures me that a garden can be both beautiful and useful.

The garden specialist whose sole aim in life is to grow one species to the zenith of perfection achieves satisfaction from the number of red cards stapled to the potting shed wall. This book is not for those who spend a lifetime seeking to know more and more about less and less. Nor is it, I suppose, for those who can co-exist with tangles of blackberry and jungles of nettles striving for supremacy with un-pruned roses and feral raspberries. I would, however, seek to share my own experience with others like myself who enjoy growing everything from alpines to forest trees, and rhubarb to asparagus, with every possible permutation between: those who look on their gardens as both an aesthetic as well as a gastronomic experience, yet enjoy the company of and seek to encourage wild creatures as well. That the cowslip gathered as a seedpod from a pasture looks perfectly at home growing alongside a Chilean fire bush in no way seems to me incongruous or out of character. Vaulting ambition is adjusted by the scissors of common sense. I have planted only precisely the number of trees which the site can support, with the exception of holly. Here I must admit to being unable to resist buying any form of native holly offered to me. The ever ready excuse is that without the holly there would be no holly blue butterflies frustrating my every effort to photograph them. Fortunately, it is less well known that this most attractive butterfly would probably be quite content with only the holly hedges and ivy of the open countryside.

The garden I set out to build and am still striving to achieve must support each and every plant which takes my fancy. Where the choice lies between one which is both beautiful and useful in conservation terms, and another which is merely handsome yet empty of other virtues, I choose the former.

There are other factors to be considered when choosing plants for a garden. The type of soil is the most important single influence, for the wise gardener selects first those plants which will grow with the minimum of cultivation while providing the maximum return. There are certain very specialised shrubs and herbs that will only thrive in soils devoid of lime. Yet it is a quite extraordinary quirk of human nature which ensures that owners of gardens where the soil is alkaline expend a lot of time and money trying to grow rhododen-drons, ling, and *camellias*. Find out first whether the soil in your plot is acid or alkaline. A simple test using one of several cheap and readily available analysis kits will quickly identify the base status of your garden soil, and what sort of plant life it will support. Do not be unduly worried if the test shows a soil heavily impregnated with lime or chalk, for under natural conditions the most interesting wild flowers are found on this type of terrain. Acid or alkaline, inner city or urban, upland or lowland the domestic garden provides a valuable haven where wildlife can enjoy a degree of immunity from pressure while still living more or less naturally. For what is natural? Perhaps only the few remnants of woodland which have not been felled and cleared for agriculture. The pattern of fields, walls and hedges is all man-made, for most of Britain, apart from marshland and mountain

Comma, red admiral and peacock butterflies on the long raceme of the 'butterfly bush', *Buddliea davidii.*

top, was covered in deciduous woodland. There were open glades filled with shrubs, wild flowers carpeting the grass: a word picture (if we include a stream or pond) which perfectly describes an ideal wild-life garden.

There is a woodland near my home which is completely natural never having been felled or interfered with. The birds, animals, and insects which abound there are precisely those commonly found in gardens. Not surprising since by planting trees, shrubs, and a lawn we create some of the conditions that prevail on a woodland edge or along the line of a centuries old hedge.

Many of the loveliest of our wild flowers can only flourish in freshly turned earth, a condition which occurs in nature very rarely. When a tree falls, river bank or cliff collapses, or grazing animals, pigs or cattle churn up the sward to expose a fresh surface to adventuring seeds. The so-called weeds of arable land (poppies are a good example), can only spread in bare disturbed soil. Again, the gardener provides this ideal habitat as a natural course. So then if the climatic climax of a Britain devoid of man is mixed woodlands, grassy glade, plus occasional plots of disturbed soil, ponds and streams, surely this more or less describes the average garden. In practical terms a garden provides a more diverse and prodigal habitat than any area of similar size allowed to form naturally. From the purely aesthetic point of view, the garden should be designed to offer a continuity of interest using flowers and fruit, so avoiding the periods of glut and famine which occur as seasonal fluctuations beyond the garden boundaries in the open countryside.

The garden habitat designed as a nature reserve can offer a greater degree of security than a wild copse or unkempt hedge. There is no risk, provided that reasonable care is taken to prevent the garden pond being polluted by toxic chemicals, nor is there the hazard to garden wildlife presented by the use of poison sprays to control weeds, pests, and diseases which increasingly threatens mass destruction of our native flora and fauna in farming areas. Add to a carefully designed plant community offering nesting facilities a variable year round food supply, supported by supplementary feeding during severe weather, and extra facilities such as drinking water, roosting and nesting boxes, and the town garden in particular will be shown to give harbourage to an astonishing range of wildlife.

One of the most rewarding aspects of a successful garden nature reserve is the opportunity it affords to observe wild animals and birds at close quarters and in intimate detail: the blackbird which nested in a tangled winter jasmine so close to a much used path that my shoulders almost brushed the brooding mother's beak; or blue tits which, in spite of my working immediately below the nest site, continued feeding hungry nestlings. Indeed, I got a very strong impression that had my mouth been open as they passed it could easily have been stuffed full of looper caterpillars! This for me is the supreme accolade, to be accepted as part of the natural scene, offering no threat to anyone or anything sharing garden space with me.

Blackbird in jasmine.

C H Gomersall (RSPB)

3. 'Treasure up your bright designs!'

Planning your garden

Planning and designing a wildlife garden is no different in most respects from fashioning a garden which will present the aesthetic qualities of plants in the best possible manner. In practice I find that a garden which suits me and is comfortable to work in makes an acceptable habitat for wildlife. There are occasions when a compromise must be reached between what is good practice in terms of soil preparation for garden, as opposed to 'wild' plants. Many of our native plants become disgustingly luxuriant of leaf and sparing in flower, when grown in a well prepared border in the garden. To accommodate plants of a spartan inclination, a corner of the lawn can be turned into a mixed meadow of native flowers and grasses. A suitable home for mountain, moorland, and downland inhabitants can be contrived by improving the drainage, then raising the level of the soil by working in heavy dressings of stone chips or coarse sand. Most gardens offer areas which even in mid summer are shaded and cool. By working in heavy dressings of peat, leaf mould, compost, or similar organic matter to improve the moisture holding capacity of the existing soil, the shade areas may be used for some of the very beautiful yet rather specialist shrubs, bulbs, and herbaceous plants which would otherwise find survival here difficult.

Possibly I am giving the impression that gardening for wildlife requires the equivalent in acres of a modest country estate to be successful. This is completely untrue as has been proved to my satisfaction on numerous occasions. Let me instance just one case, the only time I have ever been left half a garden in someone's will. The location of the house on the edge of a housing estate in the suburbs of a small town was far from ideal for the making of any type of garden. A front garden measuring 30 by 25 feet (10 by 8 metres), and a small, very shady damp plot at the rear needed a degree of faith and enthusiasm to be seen as anything other than a maternity ward for slugs, and playground for amorous cats. That the owner was partially disabled due to a spinal injury proved no deterrent. By an ingenious arrangement of troughs, raised beds, and miniscule borders there was created in the teeth of adversity a fascinating garden where native plants co-habited contentedly with others from every corner of the globe. All the wildlife was so tame, through being unmolested yet in daily contact with the gardener, it was as Eden must have been before the fall. To have a wren, of all birds, perch momentarily on my outstretched arm, was just one of many happy memories from that mini-cultivated wilderness. Spotted flycatchers with a nest of cobwebs and moss hung on a dry stone wall used the curved top of

The garden at The Croft, Didsbury, near Manchester: the RSPB's first 'home' when it was founded in 1889. Now the gardens display a fine mixture of mature trees, ornamental conifers and ground cover plants. This has the added advantage of being comparatively maintenance-free.

an eight-foot high weeping birch as a vantage point from which to waylay passing insects, tempting me to pass endless minutes just watching their fluttering aerial forays. All this and so much more achieved simply by an ingenious use of very limited space.

All the best gardens are basically very simple in design: functionally practical, while combining the three essentials of landscape trees, grass and water. Possibly I should include the boscage of shrubs, herbaceous plants, and bulbs as a fourth ingredient in the compilation of a successful habitat. There are so many factors to be considered; play areas for children, a place for drying clothes and certainly a paved area for those of us who enjoy being outdoors whenever the weather permits. Eating outside in my present garden is not without incident as one visitor discovered. He left his breakfast cereal unattended on the terrace while going indoors for a cup of tea. On returning he found a large rook busily helping itself! My pointing out that the free-loader might just have easily have been a squirrel was of little consequence.

Established gardens, in most cases, merely require supplementary and minor adjustments which I shall deal with later. First, however consider what is to most gardeners, tame or wild, the most exciting prospect of all: a new garden without grass, tree, shrub and sometimes, though perish the thought, topsoil. Let me say immediately that no-one should accept a new garden from which the topsoil has been removed without insisting that the vendor makes good the deficiency.

Never be in a hurry to rush out and plant up a new garden. This almost invariably leads to mistakes. First draw up a series of possible designs on paper locating all the features you regard as essential such as patio, terrace, play area, drying ground, greenhouse and toolshed. Make sure that all permanent items which, once installed would be difficult and extremely expensive to remove, are correctly sited. Newspapers make an easily laid substitute for paving slabs when planning the shape and extent of a terrace. A golf or sun umbrella lashed to a stake simulates a tall shrub or tree which can be tried in all the most likely vantage points to see which one is the most suitable. Once planted up, shrub borders are not easy to rearrange. In a small garden I prefer to seed the whole area down to lawn which makes cutting exactly the right shape and ratio of bed to total area much easier.

A greenhouse and shed need to be close to the house, otherwise laying on water or electricity to them becomes rather expensive. Another point often overlooked: variations in the weather often necessitate turning out late at night to adjust ventilation or check temperatures, and to have the frames or greenhouse conveniently close to the house becomes an obvious advantage. A toolshed should be adjacent to the greenhouse and house to be functional as work room and storage place. Anyone who has walked the length of the garden in a strong wind or pouring rain carrying heavy plants from potting shed to greenhouse will see the force of argument in favour of keeping these service areas in close proximity to each other.

A greenhouse needs to be in an open space away from the shade of house or trees, exposed to all the sunlight so frugally offered. Some

Water is an essential ingredient to a wildlife garden. Even a simple, shallow dish can be made to look attractive, but a home-made pool and attendant damp patch offer a delectable choice of plants and an irresistible attraction to all sorts of creatures!

shelter from the prevailing wind is advisable or heating costs soar to astronomical proportions. A carefully sited hedge or shrub border shelters by filtering the wind without shading the greenhouse.

Another important decision is how much of the garden will be given over to the cultivation of fruit and vegetables. This is one area which offers a degree of flexibility and can be expanded or contracted according to family needs. A young couple with a growing family and a limited budget would maybe devote more space to vegetables and fruit than would a retired couple. Once the trees in an orchard are established, usually by the third year, they can be grassed down. This simply means sowing the bare soil under the trees with, on a commercial orchard a grass seed mixture, whereas for a wildlife garden the seed mixture would include a selection of meadow flowers including native daffodils. Grassing down serves a dual purpose of bringing the trees into crop and making maintenance easier. In conservation terms the tree/meadow combination makes a very acceptable ornamental mini-woodland.

There is one single feature which over the years of my own gardening experience has assumed major importance, namely the pool and, if space allows, a wet place. These two provide more interest than any other single item, with the exception of a bird-table, and because of their importance need a prime situation. In my own case the pool is so situated as to be in view from certain well used rooms on the south facing front elevation, with the bird-table enjoying pride of place and the full focus of attention from the kitchen windows. Here let me make one comment regarding the siting of a bird-table. The area should consist of a broad open space, hedged in by carefully selected shrubs which are both a source of food and providers of sanctuary.

Top of my list of ideal shrubs in food, shelter, and ornamental terms, is the common holly, *Ilex aquifolium*. There are three sheltering the bird feeding ground in this garden – a plain-leaved group of male and female, plus one gold-leaved variegated female and a silver-leaved variegated male. They form a handsome, informal shelter belt which can be pruned as necessary to form an even more impenetrable barrier. In summer the scarlet flowers of *Tropaeolum* weave patterns of sprawling stems to be followed in due season by brilliant blue fruits which are guzzled by the fieldfares with the same voracity as those of the more familiar holly.

Gertrude Jekyll exhorts her readers to think of the garden as a series of rooms which, as I spend much of my time outdoors, I find to be quite an acceptable thought process. In these terms then the pool should be compared to the bathroom: it must be sheltered, reasonably quiet, yet readily accessible to all, residents and visitors alike. Ideally the pool should be kept well clear of overhanging trees, otherwise some provision has to be made to stop leaves blowing in to foul the water. Privacy can be arranged by carefully sited shrubs, or even a short run of a mixed hedge – though only on one side, for watching swallows and house martins hawking for insects over the pool is one of summer's eagerly anticipated pleasures. The pool I constructed is close planted on the north side by junipers, *Berberis*, and a short run of beech hedge.

Find space for a birdtable and you will be rewarded, especially in the winter months, with a constant stream of visitors. A birdtable can be a great source of delight, particularly for children and housebound people.

21

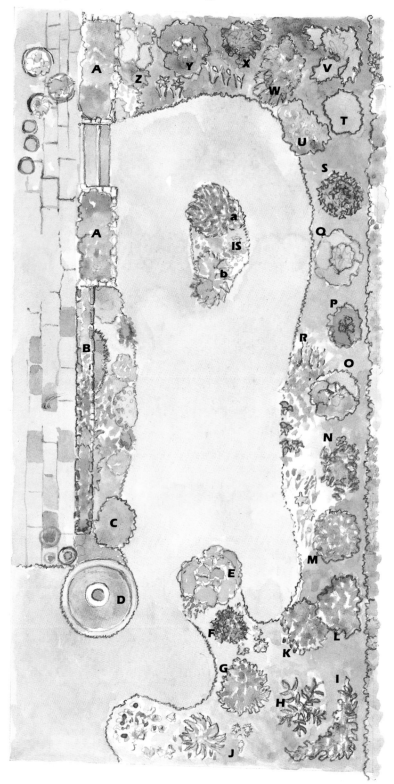

A small town garden:

A. Two raised beds containing insect-attracting plants such as thyme, *Saxifraga*, *Daphne retusa*, *Cotoneaster mic. thymifolius* and dwarf bulbs.

B. A border contains sun-loving plants such as *Helianthum alpestre*, rosemary, *Dianthus gratianopolitanus*, *Armeria*.

C. *Ozothamnus ledifolius*.

D. Bird bath with calibrated water supply to small pool.

E. *Malus x Lemoinei* underplanted with forget-me-nots and bluebells.

F. *Ilex aqu Argentia Marginata* (female) continue woodland theme with aconite and primrose.

G. *Berberis aggregata* hybs.

H. *Buddleia davidii* hybs.

I. *Cotoneaster frigidus* or *C. x wateri*.

J. *Escallonia edinensis*.

K. *Daphne mezereum* underplanted with Crocus Whitwell Purple.

L. *Clethra alnifolia*.

M. *Viburnum opulus compactum*.

N. *Hypericum* Elstead.

O. *Sorbus hybrida gibbsi* or *S. aucuparia* var. *fastigiata*.

P. Golden elder *Sambucus rac. Plumosa Aurea*.

Q. *Prunus Otto Luyken*.

R. Meadow cranesbill – loosestrife – hosta.

S. *Ilex aquifolium* with *Tropaeolum speciosum* growing through it.

T. *Amelanchier laevis*.

U. *Potentilla* K Dykes or Moonlight.

V. *Juniperus* pfitz 'Old Gold'.

W. Heathers and dwarf rhododendron if non-lime land.

X. *Mahonia japonica*.

Y. *Prunus sub Pendula Rosea* with native narcissus and snowdrop.

Z. Dwarf shrubs – *Iberis* – *Caryopteris* – *Berberis thunbergii Atropurpurea-Nana* – *Potentilla* longacre.

IS. Island bed.

a. *Cotoneaster hybridus pendulus*.

b. *Salix caprea pendula* with *Hosta sieboldii*, *Alchemilla mollis*, Geranium Mac. Ingwersen.

Fill spaces between shrubs with bulbs, annuals and herbaceous perennials. Mixed hedge behind of beech, holly, yew, thorn and cotoneaster. Lawn with curved edges and bays.

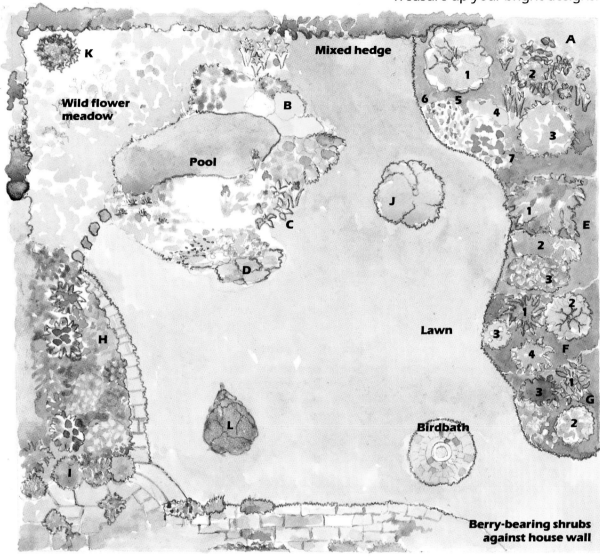

'Treasure up your bright designs!'

Plan for a garden about 50 ft (15 m) square.

A 1. *Prunus x yedoensis*; 2. *Mahonia japonica* – underplant snowdrops, *Lilium martagon*, native narcissus and winter aconite; 3. *Amelanchier laevis*; 4, 5, 6. herbaceous plants – spring, summer, autumn; 7. annuals spreading to intermingle with herbaceous plants.

B. *Hebe rakaiensis. Ulex galli* and *U. minor* compact gorse. *Cotoneaster microphyllus cochleatus et. alia.* Select Heathers according to soil.

C. Hosta, Primula, Iris, Mimulus, Caltha, Trollius, Carex, Lythrum.

D. Alpines of scree (moist) type *Saxifraga retusa, S oppositifolia, Arenaria, Phlox Douglasii* vars.

E 1. *Cotoneaster Hybridus Pendulus*; 2. *Berberis wilsoniae* or *B candidula*; 3. *Potentilla* Moonlight or

K Dykes.

F 1. *Berberis darwinii.*; 2. *Sorbus aucuparia* 'Fastigiata'; 3. *Rosa x cantabrigiensis*; 4. *Escallonia* 'Donard Radiance'.

G 1. *Buddleia* 'Lochinch'; 2. *Daphne mezereum*; 3. *Sambucus racemosa Plumosa Aurea*; ground cover of *Campanula carpatica, Hypericum olympicum.*

H. Ground cover including *Cotoneaster dammeri*, Geranium, *Astilbe chinensis pumila*, dwarf rhododendron, *Aster x Frikarti.*

I. Herbs such as Lavender, Marjoram and Hyssop.

J. *Betula pendula* 'Youngii' or male and female holly, double grafted on one stock.

K. *Crataegus monogyna* or *Oxyacantha* 'Rosea'.

L. *Chamaecy paris laws Stewartii* or *Taxus bacc. Elegantissima.*

23

The Joy of Wildlife Gardening

Contrary to the often repeated instruction that water features must be sited at the lowest point of a garden, I quite happily put them in the most convenient place. In my last garden half way up a slope, and in my present one, I have tried to emulate a typical Teesdale perched tarn hedged in with limestone pavement.

Think of the house as a focal point to the design, then in a gradual progression beginning with the terrace move through to lawns, shrub borders, and pool.

A small town garden offers a challenge and at the same time imposes a degree of restraint by reason of size. A place for sitting out which traps the sun, screened if possible to afford some privacy yet enabling a prospect of the glade formed by a shrub edged lawn. By clothing the house walls in shrubs and the trellis with climbers the immediate surrounds of the patio can be so fashioned as to afford a varied selection of nesting sites. By including also a bird-bath, fountain and a feeding-tray or table, plus additional nesting-boxes the immediate environs of the house become sufficiently well equipped to attract birds which co-exist in close proximity to human kind. Where there is only a tiny plot left once the patio is laid down, then let there be a well kept lawn surrounded by the most careful selection of bird acceptable shrubs.

To try making a wild flower lawn in such a situation of limited space is a mistake. A selection of native plants can quite easily be accommodated amongst the shrubs. I grow cowslips, meadow crane's-bill, snake's head fritillary, bird's eye primrose and harebells as ground cover under the shrubs. Choose just one shrub or small tree of suitably upright growth to add extra height and dimension to the landscape. A small upright (fastigiate) tree takes only a small amount of space whilst providing a stage for some feathered troubadour to serenade at dawn. There will be shaded areas suitable for adaptation to mini-wetlands by the skilful use of polythene liners. With care, small *can* be beautiful and it is certainly easier to maintain!

A larger garden allows the two room design of patio and mini glade to be extended. Think of the mini-glade feature as the transitional link between formal and informal. A carefully disguised path can lead through a break in the shrub planting to a tree-shaded meadow. A seat located in a corner so as to take full advantage of evening sunlight can become a pivot for the design, and make a comfortable observation post. Moss can be allowed to carpet the shaded areas, with woodland flowers in due season. If the space available for the meadow is limited, then concentrate the floral interest into one season: spring for example, could include lady's-smock, cowslip, early purple orchid, with wood anemone, violet, and marsh marigold in damper more shaded places. Once the flowers have seeded, the grass can then be mown and allowed to dry, and then turned into compost once the seed has been shed. A summer meadow is a serene place, bright with flowers of crane's-bill, knapweed, and eyebright, with all about them a busy, humming concourse of foraging insects. As for the trees, they must be in proportion to the rest of the planting. A 'meadow' measuring six by four feet (2×1·25m) would support a narrow columnar tree of no more than five to eight feet (1·7×2·5m). I would suggest one which could be kept clipped hard if necessary —

Hedgehogs are popular nocturnal visitors to my garden; they eat slugs and other less welcome creatures! Leave a few piles of leaves under the hedge or in hollows for them to hibernate in (remember to check an autumn bonfire for hibernating hedgehogs before lighting it). Hedgehogs often nest beneath a garden shed, but you could even make a hedgehog house, using an old wooden box lined with leaves or straw and placed under a suitable site such as a log pile. The entrance hole will need to be 4-5 ins (10-12 cms) square.

E H Ware (RSPB)

Fieldfares, large members of the thrush family, often come into gardens in hard weather. They, along with redwings, are winter visitors from Scandinavia, and they will feed on the berries of shrubs such as buckthorn, hawthorn and cotoneaster. Encourage them in hard weather by leaving out windfall apples and pears.

maybe an Irish yew, or one of the upright conifers with attractive foliage. *Juniperus Squamata* 'Sentinel' is useful in restricted space.

Do not for one moment presume that to make a successful wild garden the existing features have to be razed, or that an established garden is incapable of adaptation. Far from it, for unless you are so garden proud that plants are never allowed to seed, moth, nor aphid allowed to thrive, then your well-maintained plot will already be supporting some wildlife. By adding to existing features, more will be invited to share bed and board. Possibly the adaptation will be as much to the gardener's long ingrained habits and standards of routine maintenance than anything else. Meadow flowers for instance grow best in poor soil, so fertilizer must be kept off the unmown section. Instead of raking up fallen leaves for making compost let them lie as a mulch on the borders. Let the dead stems remain on herbaceous plants throughout the winter. Do not cut back dead flowers, annual or perennial, leave them to seed as a food source for goldfinches – teazels are a particular favourite. A heap of leafy prunings left under a hedge might just attract a home-hunting toad or hedgehog.

Introducing berry-bearing shrubs and nectar-rich annuals, or covering a garden shed in a tangle of creepers will all help to convert what was simply a garden into a rich and fascinating habitat.

4. Spring, that tide that leaps and swells, to bring the swallows here

Spring is not ushered in by marking a date on the calendar, nor can the season's arrival be forecast with any degree of accuracy from one year to another. For spring comes in so many different guises and we all have our own personal, intimate ways of acknowledging that the vernal season is, indeed, abroad in the land. Some will take note of aconites spreading a golden carpet of flowers as if to shame the pallid February sun. Others consider snowdrops, those 'maids of February' who hold warmth from the day in their tightly closed flowers as insulation against the chill of evening, to be the time herald of spring. Possibly it will be a blackbird practising a stanza of song like a chorister preparing for a grand opera. There are so many different ways whereby the season announces itself, always shy, hesitant, as if afraid to challenge the months long dominance of winter.

Standing in a Norfolk garden being deluged under a torrent of lark song heralded the advent of one spring. Early morning on Briet, cutting bunches of golden Soleil d' Or daffodils while a thrush drowned the quiet with melody is another. On reflection, spring is a combination of so many individual items, that, like any recipe, if one ingredient is missing then the meal is not complete. Curlews calling from the moor edge; lawn flushed with vivid green overlaying the bleached yellow; primroses clustered around the birch tree and the passionate, noisy copulation of frogs in the garden pool are all essential components. The smell of moist earth steaming gently under a sun which, free at last from the chilling east wind, is all at once benignly persuasive that growth can proceed unhindered.

I grew up in a village where respect for age and experience were accepted as an integral part of life's pattern. With the impatience of youth I wanted to be out raking soil down into a seed bed almost before the frost was properly out of the ground. The voice of reason in the shape of an elderly neighbour with experience of 60 or more seed-times restrained me. Ever since, I have heeded the advice he gave to me as a teenager – to wait until the land is steaming, or as he put it 'abrimming', and the weed seeds sprout; then and only then is it fit to sow outdoors.

In every garden I have worked there has always been a corner warmer than the rest, a sheltered place which gathers and holds sunshine as a miser hoards gold. By careful planning it is possible to contrive a welcome show of spring flowers earlier than would be feasible anywhere else in the garden. My spring corner is near the pool, facing due south, and sheltered from the north by shrubs, on the east by a spreading *Juniperus x media* 'Pfitzeriana' and the stone-

J V and J R Harrison (Aquila)

With the lengthening hours of daylight, the birds soon start courting. The garden robin (left) sings to proclaim his territory and the first flowers start to bloom – one of my favourite spring flowers is the primrose (above).

parapetted well. First to flower are aconites, snowdrops and tiny *Narcissus asturiensis* from northern Spain, with a carpet of red flowered *Saxifraga oppositifolia* – all native or naturalised except the daffodil. A dwarf willow is included to give height and a certain pastoral restraint. In 20 years, *Salix x boydii* has grown to only 15 inches (38 cm), yet presents authentic 'pussy willow' catkins for Palm Sunday. As the season progresses, cowslips, gorse, the lovely lavender-blossomed *Primula farinosa*, and pale purple crocus take the stage to witness the festival of frogs' matrimony and birth at one and the same time.

Crocus are important in that they beautify the garden while providing brood food to foraging bees. Usually, when the quince, *Chaenomeles* 'Knap Hill Scarlet' shows flower buds, I notice the blue tits busy about the hole left for the purpose in the garage wall. That they, in recognition of my hospitality carefully snip off the quince flowers then drop them under the birch tree is another of spring's tokens, and a hint to stop filling up the peanut dispensers.

Imperceptibly, the tempo of life quickens. As the days lengthen so there is opportunity to work in the garden for an hour or two each evening. Once again the voice of the lawnmower is heard in the land. First, however, give the lawn a thorough raking to clear away the debris of winter. This is particularly important if young children or a dog are part of the menage. A half chewed bone or piece of Meccano can play havoc with newly sharpened lawnmower blades, not to mention family harmony! Birds show their approval of this annual grooming by searching the scarified turf for grubs, and gathering moss and dead grass for nest building.

There will be clearing up to be done amongst herbaceous plants. Dead stems must be cut away before the new shoots grow up amongst them. The pruning away of last year's dead stems is particularly important on early flowering herbaceous plants; *Euphorbia polychroma*, for example, pushes up blossoming shoots at an alarming rate as the weather warms.

Before the soil dries out to provide the seed bed peck of dust I get a moisture-conserving mulch onto shrub borders and rose beds. This is good both in gardening terms as a means of improving the soil, and as a habitat it acts as a substitute for forest leaf litter which serves as a breeding ground for insects and, consequently, a food source for birds.

Preparations need to be set in hand during early April for sowing hardy annual flower seeds later in the month. No matter how well the garden may be provided with a continuity of flowers from shrub and herbaceous plants, annuals are an essential supplement because they flower during the summer and autumn, the peak period of insect activity and nestling feeding time. Plants that set seed form a link in the food chain, as those who include sunflowers, teasel and poppy as a regular part of the spring sowing will appreciate.

A good deal of the work expended on the vegetable garden is concentrated into the April-May-June period in a mayhem of raking, sowing and planting. By working the soil twice I create a fine tilth for seed sowing, while offering the birds easy access to soil-borne pests like cutworm, wireworm, and other noxious beings.

Spring, that tide that leaps and swells

Top fruit will all be pruned, fed, and mulched at this time though a watchful eye needs to be kept on gooseberries to prevent bullfinches plundering the growth buds. Damage to ornamental plants is severe when the hawthorn, the birds' first choice, is late into growth due to unfavourable weather. In a cold, wet spring, I net gooseberry and damson as a precaution.

To work in a garden through the long hours of a spring day is to share in part, the miracle of a new creation. The upsurge of growth is so apparent as to be almost a visible presence, and the busy life of bird and insect gathers force and meaning from the sun's increasing warmth. I am fortunate that all the spring times of my working life have been spent working in garden or woodland, so that every subtle change can be noted and savoured to the full. To see a newly constructed nesting box being investigated by home hunting tits within hours of installation offers sufficient excuse for a pause from work to see if they find the accommodation suitable.

Spring is such a shy, elusive and unqualified alchemy of sights, sounds, shades and scents that it is never a continuous progression, so unless you allow time to become absorbed in the pattern of the season, many of the subtle shifts and changes will be missed. These are moments to cherish in memory. I was standing on the Point at Blakeney on the north Norfolk coast, when a huge charm of goldfinches flew in across the estuary to settle on the bushes all around me. For a brief moment I was witness to the miracle of migration, for I could sense through the birds an all-compelling urgency. Of the largest concourse of hares I have ever seen, there must have been 20 or more all filled with March madness which for a brief season turns a solitary, timid beast into a gyrating, punching, kicking termagant.

Quiet moments there are also, when at dawn the garden belongs to the early risers – birds and other animals, and some humans. Then again in late evening as darkness grows out of the shadows cast by the hedge to cover the whole garden.

There is also the joy of seeing some plant grown from seed in flower for the first time. Last year it was a white-flowered snake's head fritillary, the only one amongst a colony of the purple petalled type which I had sown four years previously. The seed, sent to me from an Oxford garden, came from native stock and was treasured accordingly. Minor triumphs, those serenely satisfying moments that linked together form the rich pattern of spring, are memories in a gardener's almanac.

Peter Hinchliffe (Bruce Coleman Ltd)

The marsh tit knows that hiding under the leaf litter is a host of small invertebrate creatures.

5. The populous and fertile earth

Understanding your garden's soil and some of the creatures that inhabit it

Now is the time to deal with the nature of different soils, the strength and colour of each, and their quotient fertility. For Virgil had it right in his assertion that soils vary widely in character while still needing similar basic cultivations to bring them into cropping. I doubt that dream of poets and planners of factories in the fields has found expression in modern farming practice, where good husbandry begins not so much with the soil as in a chemist's shop.

For if the garden in plain view appears a populous place, then the top four inches (10 cms) of soil which is out of sight positively heaves with activity. At least this is so in a healthy soil, well supplied with organic matter, and where chemicals are used only as a last resort not as a routine corrective for bad husbandry. Some understanding of the composition and structure of soil, together with an appreciation of the interdependence of life above and below the surface makes for a clearer awareness of what a balanced habitat means.

Some of the soil inhabitants: slugs, snails, roundworms, earthworms, insects, spiders, woodlice, millipedes, centipedes, beetles, and many others are large enough to be identified. They can then be categorised as friend, foe, or neutral. Some vertebrates, moles for example, are friends when they devour soil pests, and enemies when they heave up mini-Everests in the lawn or newly sown vegetable plot.

Soils can be roughly classified for gardening purposes as light, medium, or heavy – a judgement arrived at according to the proportion of sand or clay in their composition. Soils derived from the limestone or chalk will as a rule be defined as alkaline. Others formed from sandstone, millstone grit, and other non-alkaline rock structures will be neutral or acid in reaction. A soil's basic status, whether acid or alkaline, can be measured by various means – the results are usually expressed in terms of a pH scale. A neutral soil has a pH of 7·0. Any reading above that figure is described as alkaline. One would expect a soil containing small amounts of free lime to have a pH of 7·5. Conversely, a reading of pH 6·5 would indicate an acid soil. Increased acidity would be expressed on a descending scale: 6, 5, 4, and alkalinity on an ascending scale; 7, 8, 9. Any soil which is being cultivated will tend to become acid, and especially so when heavy dressings of farm manure or peat are being applied. For most gardeners it is sufficient to know that a simple test will identify whether their soil is acid and suitable for the cultivation of lime-hating plants like rhododendrons, or limey, in which case it is better to grow lime-tolerant flora only. For most gardening purposes a soil with a pH

The Joy of Wildlife Gardening

reading of 6·5-7 (neutral) is ideal, allowing as it does the widest possible range of plants to be grown.

Let us turn from the Utopian subject of ideal pH, to another, namely the best soil to work with. My choice would be for a medium to heavy loam, free-draining yet containing enough organic matter (humus) to prevent excessive drying out, and of a rich dark brown colour so it warms up quicky in spring. I have never achieved the ideal, but all soils, no matter what their condition, can be improved if properly worked. There are no better aids in this respect than a spade and compost heap. These, used with the prime qualifications of a gardener (as outlined by the first head gardener I worked under), namely 'a strong back and a weak head', are the recipe for a contented lifestyle.

Soils which contain larger than average amounts of clay, the 'heavy soils' in gardening terminology, are potentially very fertile. They are difficult to work, hold excessive proportions of water and bake like bricks, rather than crumbling, when dry. Opening up the sub-soil and working in generous dressings of organic matter into the top 10 inches (25 cm) will gradually, if repeated annually, improve the quality of clay soil. I worked a glacial clay soil for 20 years: after the first five it would grow almost any crop well. Working in coarse sand or chippings will improve the physical structure and snould be used on clay soils in conjunction with the organic dressings.

At the other extreme are the light soils which contain a large proportion of sand particles. These drain quickly, are easy to work even after heavy rain, and warm up early in spring. They are hungry because nutriments, either organic or applied as bag manure, soon leach out, whereas in a heavy soil the clay fraction holds chemical elements firmly against being washed out. Light land is also the first to suffer from drought. Medium loams with every variation of colour and texture bridge the gap between the extremes of clay and sand. The peatlands of the Fens (East Anglia) are a product of a condition where land long under water was then drained, exposing what is virtually a slowly decomposing compost heap to light and air.

All soils are improved by dressings of organic matter whether they are light or heavy, peat or plain, acid or alkaline providing, of course, they are not waterlogged. Excessive acidity can have a harmful effect on plant growth and this can be corrected by a dressing of lime or chalk. Incidentally, a dressing of lime at regular intervals, usually every three years, will greatly improve the workability of a heavy soil by causing the clay molecules to gather together and form crumbs. The term used to describe this function is flocculation. Supplementary feeding may occasionally be necessary, especially of intensively culti-vated fruit or vegetables.

Plants require three essential elements to maintain balanced and healthy growth. The first is nitrogen, for leaf and stem: unfortunately, this is an element which dissolves readily in water and is, therefore, quickly washed out of the soil. The second is phosphate. This is vital to plants in the seedling stage to promote healthy root growth. Potash is the third major plant food in that it promotes flower and fruit pro-duction, improving their colour and flavour. Potash can also be used to correct the soft growth of stem and leaf due to an over-indulgence in nitrogen.

Nowhere is the ecological balance – the relationship between flora, fauna, and the environment – more finely balanced or easily disrupted, than in the soil. Once the stability is upset by pollution, incorrect cultivation, or exploitation, restoring the original healthy state of affairs may be at best a long term process, or in extreme cases impossible. A valley which I have known since childhood is a graphic example of this. In five years, the stripping of natural vegetation, and over-grazing, have resulted in gully erosion in the worst affected areas, and a serious reduction in fertility over a considerable area.

In addition to minerals and organic matter in various stages of decay, the soil contains and provides sustenance for a thriving population of insects, fungi, bacteria, worms, mammals, gastropods, and others. These in turn are a source of food in a chain of inter-dependence which leads ultimately to cabbage consuming, meat-eating man.

The most important soil inhabitant, according to authorities of the calibre of Charles Darwin and Gilbert White of Selborne, is the earthworm (*Lumbricus*). Certainly, the song thrush, with legs braced and straining every sinew to extract a worm from the lawn at this very moment, would subscribe to that. Judging by the size of the said worm, I suspect the other end is somewhere deep in Loch Ness! One can get some idea of the power of an earthworm by catching a worm half into its burrow by its 'tail'. The odds are that the worm will escape and the strength displayed is an essential asset for a creature which spends its life tunnelling in the soil. The worm by its activities improves soil aeration and drainage. Worms also enrich the soil by swallowing earth, then digesting the animal and plant remains it contains. Nowhere is worm activity more apparent than in the lawn as witness the casts spread over the surface during mild, wet weather. Most beneficial also, which is why I never use worm killers on any lawn in my care.

Snails and slugs are other familiar, usually maligned denizens of the garden. A snail's body is in two main sections: the foot is the means of locomotion and has the head at one end, and the second section or visceral hump, holds vital organs safely tucked away in the shell. Some slugs are flesh eaters, but the majority, as the gardener knows only too well, are vegetarians feeding on both living and dead organic material. Two species only, the garden and strawberry snails, are serious garden pests. Thrushes are useful allies in our struggle to reduce the snail population.

Slugs are amongst the most destructive of garden pests. That they are shell-less snails which have packed all their working parts (including a substantial stomach) into the foot/head is no consolation. Being shell-less, they protect themselves with a slimey mucus which often betrays their presence to the gardener. Of the dozen or so slug species which frequent gardens, there are slugs which still have shells. One of these has the shell perched like an afterthought near the tail, and is carnivorous, feeding largely on earthworms. Fortunately, slugs are eagerly hunted as food by toads, some birds, and more especially, hedgehogs, which guzzle them with audible relish. Hedgehogs are not too selective in their eating habits and will gobble up slugs which have been killed with poison bait, so where possible avoid using

Song thrush with earthworm. One of the most important animals to the earth's natural cycle is the humble earthworm. There are several thousand different species of earthworm, and about 24 species are found in the British Isles. They are omnivorous, eating their way inexorably through living and decaying plant material, microscopic animals and animal faeces. As well as providing a continuous supply of humus, they fulfil an essential function in aerating the soil, and are themselves valuable food for birds and mammals such as moles, shrews, even foxes and badgers.

The Joy of Wildlife Gardening

pellets which could prove toxic to more than gastropods.

Woodlice, like mini-armadillos, used to fascinate me when I was a child, possibly it was the discovery that they belong to the same class as crabs and other crustaceans which stimulated my interest. This also explained why they were only found in damp corners, under stones, rotting logs, or wall crevices. They can be a nuisance in fruit houses or when given access to tender young seedlings, yet they perform a useful service in helping to break down rotting vegetation. Shrews are great woodlice killers: the greenhouse toad relishes them too, so next time a boot is raised to tread on a woodlouse (which seems to be a first instinct for most gardeners), pause, you could be squashing a toad's breakfast. *Onisais asellus* is the commonest species of wood-louse to be found in gardens.

The multi-legged millipede, and the closely related *Scutigerella*, can be quite a serious nuisance in greenhouses in which bedding plants are being raised. Outside, the black and snake millipedes are the most commonly encountered. In dry summers they may damage root crops in their search for moisture. Other species assist in the breakdown of plant debris, so not all millipedes are villains, and like almost everything else in the garden they are hunted by shrews, hedgehogs, spiders, and; I suspect, centipedes with which they are sometimes confused.

Though long and slender like the millipede, centipedes only have one pair of legs to each body segment (millipedes have two) and are very mobile – as predators, they need to be. Centipedes eat slugs and a vast array of other soil fauna including, unfortunately, some which are allies of the husbandman, especially worms. Under a hand lens the venom claws are revealed as fearsome weapons. Like woodlice, millipedes and centipedes thrive only in moist conditions for they are not well protected against dehydration.

The turf and upper layers of the soil contain a host of creatures that provide food for birds and other wildlife: earthworm, banded and kentish snails, woodlouse and large black slugs.

Mike Langman (after original by Rob Shepperson)

34

Spiders are familiar creatures living alongside man in both house and garden. That they can also be a fascinating study in themselves is something I discovered in my boarding school days when a degree of discipline was introduced into my all-consuming interest in biology. The various species which advertise their presence by building webs attract most attention. Others, like the crab spider, lurk in amongst leaves or even inside flowers, ready to seize insects attracted to them. Wolf spiders, long-legged and fleet of foot, run their prey down, while zebra or jumping spiders rely on stealth to get within pouncing distance of lunch.

Harvestmen flourish in an undisturbed corner of the garden. The very long legs with the body slung between them topped by periscope eyes are characteristic of these very useful pest controllers. They will eat caterpillars, root aphids, and a whole range of pests. In my garden they are particularly abundant amongst the lady's mantle which provides a reservoir of moisture in the cupped leaves, for harvestmen are dependent on easy access to moisture or they quickly dehydrate and perish.

Beetles are one of the familiar, easily identified denizens of the soil. I say easily recognised only in terms that they are beetles; telling the various species apart is an altogether different matter. Click beetles (*Elateridae*) are possibly the most important, and are easily identified by just turning them on their backs. They arch themselves, and with a clearly audible click are projected into the air to land the right way up, though not always at the first attempt. Click beetles are the adult phase of the pestilential wireworms which spend three, four, or five years in the soil feeding on plant roots and other organic matter. In spite of a very tough covering wireworms are eagerly sought after as a gourmet delicacy by birds and other animals in our gardens.

Maybugs or cockchafers which blunder around on June evenings like aerial dodgems, bumping into anything in their way, are a major pest both in the larval and adult phases. The larvae are fat and greyish in colour with a brown head: they spend several years feeding on plant roots while the adults are similarly occupied eating leaves above ground. Garden chafers have adopted much the same life style. Fortunately, the fat, juicy grubs are avidly sought after by a whole legion of predators, both biped and quadruped so are a valuable link in the food chain. Small consolation this is to the gardener, but rooks and starlings find them irresistible.

Crane flies, the 'daddy-long-legs' of our childhood, are a familiar sight about the garden with their frenetic buzzing and jerky flight. They are particularly evident on lawns in August when egg laying. These eggs hatch in the fullness of time into one of the most pernicious garden pests: leatherjackets. Their depredations are largely confined to lawns where the brownish yellow larvae feed on the grass roots often in such numbers as to cause large yellow patches. One of the pleasures to be savoured, is of pied wagtails scurrying around like busy clockwork toys hunting the crane flies at egg-laying time.

Various flies occupy a place in the garden, though few are dependent on the soil at any stage in their life cycle. Some, such as the soldier flies, vinegar flies and the like, or fungus gnats are found on manure

The Joy of Wildlife Gardening

heaps or near piles of decomposing vegetation as the wrens and dunnocks in this garden very obviously are well aware. Some, such as the stilt fly (*Trepidaria*), breed in decaying vegetation, then as adults prey on greenfly. Others like the carrot and celery flies are a serious pest of vegetable crops in the larval stage. Still, what is lost on the swings is gained on the roundabouts: flies, gnats and gall midges which hatch in their millions from soil, compost heap, and hedgerow are a vital link in the food chain for birds, for without them how would swallows, swifts and house martins feed their hungry broods?

Bees and wasps can hardly be called creatures of the soil being more things of the air, part of warm summer days and nectar-rich flowers. Because bumble bees, those most attractive pollen seekers, nest in holes self-excavated or left by other burrowers, as do solitary bees, their inclusion in the semi earth-dependent class is only proper. Bees are vital agents in the reproductive cycle of many flowers: they transfer pollen, without which no seed would set to ensure the procreation of future generations. We can, of course, ensure a sufficiency of bees for pollinating purposes by introducing a hive of honey bees, though in a small town garden this could be considered anti-social. Many people classify all wasps and bees as dangerous creatures which sting, so would-be apiarists be warned.

Wasps come in varying shapes: some, like the digger wasp, which throw up mounds of sandy soil between the crevices of the paving on my laboriously-constructed terrace, look more like blackflies than wasps. Some gather aphids to store in underground cells as food for hatching grubs, so are an unpaid pest control to be encouraged. The most familiar wasps are, however, the brown and yellow striped variety who are often inadvertently discovered half buried in a ripe plum, or helping themselves to the jam at a picnic. They fashion nests of paper made from chewed wood, and in spite of their stings really are a first class pest control to be succoured not destroyed, for the

Centipede, leatherjacket (the larvae of the cranefly), millipede, violet ground beetle, devil's coach-horse, black ants and money spiders.

Mike Langman (after original by Rob Shepperson)

36

larvae are fed on caterpillars and greenfly.

Ants are soil-dependent even though many make nests under paving stones, others build mounds or excavate burrows under lawns to live completely subterranean existences. Ants feed on a variety of plant and animal material, they also farm aphids; a rather reprehensible practice. They do, however form an important link in the food chain. I have watched green woodpeckers foraging for them many times. They must also be eaten in prodigious quantities by hawking birds when whole nests of males and queen ants take wing in great swarms to mate.

Sawflies, ladybirds, and ichneumon flies, the preyed on and predator, the living threads of a closely woven tapestry which spreads a mantle over the garden. Small suburban plot, balcony garden, window box, each a small part of the interlocking living fabric which together forms a vital habit. Without them our towns would become lifeless, polluted, sterile wastelands.

In addition to containing decaying animal and plant material, the soil supports a vast concourse of visible life forms. All healthy soil, undisturbed or cultivated, seethes with life when viewed through a microscope. Under even modest magnification a vast population of fungi and bacteria is revealed which under normal conditions coexist in well-balanced harmony: those beneficial numerous enough to control those which cause disease. The gardener's aim is to maintain and enhance this very desirable state of affairs by correct cultivation. A soil which is in poor physical condition due to over-compaction, waterlogging, or continuous over-cropping, will fall into imbalance with diseases like club root of brassica, or pests like potato root eelworm proliferating. By improving drainage, aeration, and fertility of the soil, and practising crop rotation the healthy balance between beneficial micro organisms and those which are harmful will be restored. An excessive use of soil pesticides and fungicides may control the nuisance, though frequently only in the short term. In the long term, by seriously depleting beneficial soil organisms the cure may even compound the problem.

The normal routine of digging, composting, and irrigation improves soil aeration, provides a breeding ground for essential organisms, and helps to free essential plant nutrients.

Soil left undisturbed in its natural vegetated state will be self-maintaining, the chemical and physical structure being maintained by the decay of plant and animal remains. Under cultivation the uptake of nutrients is accelerated to such a degree that unless they are replenished with regular dressings of organic matter soil structure and fertility will be seriously reduced. The direct application of synthetic chemicals useful to the plant will support crops but at the same time will reduce in a dramatic and alarming fashion the usefulness of the soil as provider of sustenance to birds, animals, and insects. Without a healthy soil teeming with an abundance of life, both visible and invisible, no garden can ever make even a token pretence of being a wildlife habitat. The gardener who said 'everything begins with the soil' deserves better than to become the butt of less visionary humorists.

6. 'Down the hedge they hop and hide'

Making your garden secluded and safe for wildlife

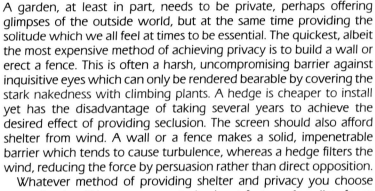

A garden, at least in part, needs to be private, perhaps offering glimpses of the outside world, but at the same time providing the solitude which we all feel at times to be essential. The quickest, albeit the most expensive method of achieving privacy is to build a wall or erect a fence. This is often a harsh, uncompromising barrier against inquisitive eyes which can only be rendered bearable by covering the stark nakedness with climbing plants. A hedge is cheaper to install yet has the disadvantage of taking several years to achieve the desired effect of providing seclusion. The screen should also afford shelter from wind. A wall or a fence makes a solid, impenetrable barrier which tends to cause turbulence, whereas a hedge filters the wind, reducing the force by persuasion rather than direct opposition.

Whatever method of providing shelter and privacy you choose remember it will be a permanent, dominant feature. A wall or fence can be transformed into something beautiful by a covering of vegetation. A hedge which is a living part of the garden is equally appealing.

Wall shrubs need pruning, tying, and feeding, but then so will a hedge if it is to continue to grow well. A shrub-covered wall offers shelter and potential nesting sites as well as flowers and berries. In fact, it can be as rich and diverse a habitat as a hedge. Once again, the whole question of choice is decided by how much we can afford to pay, in association with other factors such as local soil conditions.

My own garden and conservation experience includes firsthand knowledge of walled gardens, fences and hedges. The ideal, of course, is a combination of a hedge set some 15 feet (five metres) in front of a wall which affords shelter to temper even a force nine gale. Lest anyone whisper 'impractical ideal', I worked in such a garden in the Yorkshire dales 1,000 feet (300 metres) above sea level. There, plums, cherries, apples, and other epicurean delights ripened in the micro-climate enclosed within the wall boundaries.

Let us look first at the hedges which best fulfil the triple purpose of furnishing shelter, privacy, and a wide spectrum habitat. In the open countryside, hedges form a network linking together the richly patterned landscape in such a way as to enhance its overall beauty. The composition of hedges varies: in southern Britain, spindle, hazel, field maple, oak, *Clematis*, *Viburnum*, sweet chestnut, and dogwood mix with the cosmopolitan hawthorn which binds all together. In the northern counties holly, elder, blackthorn, blackberry, dog rose, crab apple and honeysuckle pleach with hawthorn to make long trodden drove roads and green lanes.

The Joy of Wildlife Gardening

A hedge is shelter not only for a rich variety of birds and animals but for flowers and insects too. Celandines along with wood violets begin a continuous succession of flowers, all handsome enough to adorn a garden. Add to these primrose, bluebell, meadow crane's-bill, giant bellflower, herb Robert and the creamy foamed lace of cow parsley, and a picture is the result. Insects swarm to plunder the flowers. Birds abound, for hedges provide safe nesting sites and the abundance of insects, nuts, berries and fruit, forms an ever-replenished larder. Wood mice and bank voles hunt for food and are themselves hunted. Frogs, toads, and omnivorous hedgehogs all explore the hedge line. In so many memories of my childhood experiences, the hedge, bordering a country lane, features prominently. I vividly recall discovering the first flowers of spring, counting nests, picking hazelnuts or blackberries, and gathering crab apples in October to make the amber-coloured jelly which marries so perfectly with fresh scones.

In practical terms, any shrub which will stand being clipped without suffering discomfort can be trained to form a hedge. Monoculture, the planting of just a single species is the commonly accepted practice when putting down a hedge. Beech, yew, *Cupressocyparis leylandii*, hawthorn, and holly all make excellent hedges either singly or in combination. The contribution a single species hedge can make is limited: it can provide shelter, privacy, nesting sites, and a modest though rigidly seasonal food supply. But a mixed hedge can, if the shrubs in its composition are selected with care, grow to become at least the equal of a field hedge in the variety of flora and fauna happy to live in association with it, providing a much greater resource to wildlife, and variety and interest in a single feature for the gardener.

There is no disadvantage in using shrubs which need pruning in different months providing none require trimming during the busy nesting season. Several of the barberries provide flowers and berries in abundance together with the sort of secure nest sites which long-tailed tits and goldfinches prefer. *Berberis darwinii* is a superb evergreen growing to six feet (two metres) high, and *Berberis stenophylla* is a thicket forming, suckering bush which makes a dense barrier. *Berberis thunbergii* is also popular because there are varieties which grow fiercely upright in both red and green leaved forms. A mixture of *Berberis thunbergii* types using 'Erecta' and 'Red Pillar' mixed in with the green-leaved species forms a colourful five to six feet (two metres) high hedge. *Cotoneaster simonsii* is used as a fringe planting to pheasant coverts because the profusion of berries become available shortly after the birds are released. Used as a component of a garden hedge, the erect habit and orange scarlet berries are both useful and ornamental.

Amongst the 'firethorns' (*Pyracantha*) there is an almost bewildering selection. A mixture of yellow and orange fruiting varieties affords an interesting study, for the red and orange berries are eaten by the birds almost immediately they are ripe, whereas the yellow fruits remain on the bushes for months. Pruning of all berrying shrubs, including holly, consists of trimming back current season's growth to leave the fruits exposed.

Roses are frequently used to form ornamental hedges, though

A blackcap eating elderberries. Early autumn berries are a vital source of food to many of our small summer-visiting birds, especially warblers, which will feed heavily on them to ensure they have sufficient body fuel to undertake the long migratory journey.

'Down the hedge they hop and hide'

Eric Hosking

Berries are also important for our winter visitors, like these redwings feasting on Pyracantha. I have noticed red and orange Pyracantha berries seem to be eaten before the yellow-berried variety.

usually the varieties chosen are selected for flower quality only. The gardener who is concerned with husbanding wildlife should consider instead roses which carry heavy crops of hips into the autumn. Various forms of *Rosa rugosa* offer interesting variations in flower colour and hip shape and grow to six feet (about two metres) in height. Also, the Penzance briars with fragrant foliage, single flowers and colourful hips, though possibly best grown on a trellis, will, if pruned regularly make a good, rough hedge associating well with holly, hawthorn, and honeysuckle.

The permutations which can be worked using native shrubs along with those introduced from abroad, form an interesting field worthy of investigation. For the gardener, the prime advantage of a mixed, as opposed to a monoculture hedge, is that new species can be planted to mingle with those already established at any time, as opportunity or fancy dictates. Frequently birds assist the process of integration by depositing seeds, so that the number of species builds up precisely as they will over the passage of years in a field hedge. That was how elderberry, that most useful hedgerow shrub, came into my garden: via a loose-bowelled bird. Dunnocks and wrens are avid hedge-hunters. Dunnocks search for insects in spring and summer, then change to a diet of seeds in autumn. Wrens are, of course, insect

41

eaters which hunt near the ground like busy, feathered, noisily scolding shrews.

Greenfinches are compulsive hedge-nesters. Those in my garden have also acquired the annoying habit of eating *Daphne* berries while they are still green, which prevents any natural regeneration from self-sown seedlings. Bullfinches, which plunder the buds on gooseberries, damson plums, and many ornamentals, also nest in dense hedges. Their presence is a mixed blessing in that they take heavy toll of insect pests when feeding their young.

A hedge is, or should be, a permanent feature, so make sure that the soild has been thoroughly prepared before a single item is planted. I trench the hedge line, digging a strip four feet (just over a metre) wide along the full length to a depth of 18 inches (about a half a metre). Remove all perennial weeds and mix in rotted manure, compost or any organic matter at the same time. Removing weeds may seem a contradiction, but failure to do so will result in a weed-infested, impossible-to-live-with rubbish heap. To be fully effective a conservation garden needs maintenance and the same degree of commitment as a formal plot. Species are introduced on our terms as the need for them becomes evident. Anyone with a 'deck chair and let nature take its course' approach would be well advised to plant the garden with a load of ready-mixed cement!

Not all garden boundaries are marked with a hedge. Fences of wood, wire, plastic, and stone walls serve a similar purpose; that of marking the limits of our authority. Do make certain any wood used for fencing has not been treated with a preservative harmful to plant-life but with a preservative such as Cuprinol or Woody.

Walls provide shelter and in consequence a degree or two of extra warmth: this means that shrubs can be accommodated which would otherwise find our climate too harsh to be tolerable.

Many plants come ready-provided with a natural means of supporting themselves. Ivy (*Hedera*), Boston ivy (*Parthenocissus tricuspidata*), and climbing *Hydrangea* (*Hydrangea petiolaris*) are examples of plants which scramble up walls by means of adhesive pads, tendrils, or aerial roots.

Other so-called climbers will need support to provide something for the stems to twine through or be tied onto. One method is an open trellis made from wood or plastic fitted to wooden bobbins screwed to the wall. Brackets firmly screwed to the wall or fence spaced 12 inches (30 cm) apart with plastic-covered wire stretched between, is just as effective. I was preparing a wall here for planting climbing roses by fitting a wooden trellis, and in the interval between preparation and actual rose planting a blackbird nested between trellis and wall. I planted the rose and tied shoots onto the trellis watched by a totally unconcerned but very interested brooding hen blackbird. While functioning reasonably well when trained across a wall, roses do look best when grown as they do naturally over a bank or scrambling over a shrub or into a tree. The banksian rose (*Rosa banksiae* 'lutea'), *R. filipes* 'Kiftsgate', and *R. multiflora* are examples of the scrambler roses.

Roses constrained on a wall need to be of the type which respond to pruning if they are to flower well. 'Albertine', with salmon-pink

Greenfinches huddle together, preparing to roost. A good thick hedge will be a boon for roosting birds in winter.

flowers will comfortably cover 12 square feet (1·5 square metres) of wall space, whereas 'Handel' with creamy white flowers edged cherry-pink will be content with only half that area. For many years I grew the bright pink, thornless and fragrant *Zépherine Drouhin* over a porch pergola, and each spring a blackbird nested in the lacework of branches. Roses are so personal that selection is a matter of individual taste.

Ceanothus are made up of mostly evergreen shrubs which at least in the colder districts are best accommodated on a wall. There, the bright blue-purple or pink flowers are produced in abundance to the benefit of bees and other insects.

Clematis, apart from those which flourish on a minimum of pruning, are not especially important contributors except in the matter of beautiful flowers. There are exceptions, particularly the notoriously rampant forms of *Clematis montana*. I have a specimen of *C. montana* 'Elizabeth' growing over an apple tree a 10 feet (three metres) high mound of pink flowers in May, and a popular maternity ward each year for dunnock, thrush, and wren.

Consideration of a climber's qualities in wildlife terms, instead of merely ornamental attributes, adds greater interest to designing a garden. There are certain situations requiring what, for want of a better word, I would describe as specialist plants: for north facing walls or other shady areas. Taking into account merely ornamental value there is plenty of choice including ivy, climbing *Hydrangea*, *Pyracantha*, *Camellia*, *Cotoneaster*, *Euonymus*, *Jasminium*, Morello cherry and possibly a dozen other shrubs able to adjust to poor light conditions. Add to the qualifications the proviso that they must also be complementary to a wildlife habitat and the choice is much reduced. All will offer nesting facilities to some degree, but only *Cotoneaster*, ivy, *Pyracantha*, and Morello cherries supply a spring and autumn food source too. Indeed, a Morello cherry grew along the north side of a barn in my first garden. During May the profusion of white blossom was like drifting snow, and this was followed in due season by great clusters of fruit which when fully ripe made a delicious dessert. Unfortunately, the blackbirds shared my appreciation and guzzled the cherries even as they took on the first flush of pale pink, when to a real connoisseur they were still inedible.

Ivy is of particular value as the flowers open in October to provide a food source that wasps and other insects are quick to exploit. Ivy is of course a host to the caterpillars of the holly blue butterfly. I have also seen beaded chestnut moths feeding on ivy blossom in mid-October — a most intriguing inducement to time-wasting. By choosing various forms of common ivy which have variegated foliage it is possible to arrive at a handsome tapestry effect of gold, silver and pale green.

In addition to *C. simonsii* which I mentioned as suitable hedging material, the *Cotoneasters* offer better value both as conservation and ornamental shrubs than any other single genus. The most widely grown is possibly the herringbone-patterned *C. horizontalis*. I grow it on a north wall and to prop up a decrepit dry stone dyke where as food source and nesting site it is invaluable. For wall cultivation, the evergreen *C. salicifolius*, parent of innumerable hybrids, is outstand-

Small mammals, like wood mice and weasels, will use a hedge as a 'roadway'. Trim a hedge once a year, aiming for an 'A' shape, with a dense, wide base. January is probably the best time for trimming: before the birds start nesting and after the berries have been eaten. When planting a hawthorn hedge, hard prune the plants back almost to the ground to encourage growth at the bottom.

ingly good. I know of a house wall some 20 feet (six metres) high which is covered in a network of this attractive species. In autumn, as the berries ripen the waxwings appear as if by prior invitation to feed on them. I have often wondered how birds and other animals get news of seasonal food supplies like this.

By offering a richly varied bill of fare it is surprising just how many different bird species are attracted to a small garden. One of the loveliest twining plants in my opinion is our native honeysuckle which, fortunately, features prominently along the lane verges in my neighbourhood. To sit enjoying the fragrance distilled by those honeygold, purple flushed flowers while watching hawkmoths feeding on the nectar is a proper reward for those who cultivate *Lonicera periclymenum*. A mistake often made when planting honeysuckle in the garden is to make the soil too rich when in nature it seems to prefer quite dry, acid loams well supplied with leaf mould.

Several years ago there was, in the Norfolk garden owned by one of my aunts, a most ugly shed which I suggested disguising behind a canopy of climbers. I planted honeysuckle, *Clematis montana*, and Russian vine (*Polygonum baldschuanicum*) and within three years, the shed had disappeared under a tangle of stems. The variety of birds which nested there was more diverse than I would have believed possible in so small an area. That anyone needing to get into the shed had to carry a pair of secateurs with them because the Russian vine grew so vigorously, was a minor inconvenience.

There are other common climbers; white and black bryony, hop, woody nightshade, great bindweed and traveller's joy which, though beautiful when lacing a field hedge, are over invasive to be considered as garden plants. Some climbers, such as woody nightshade, produce appetising red berries which are poisonous, so should be excluded on that score if children have access to the garden.

As to the ubiquitous bramble there will be no question of whether to incorporate this particular scrambler into the design, as the birds will provide both means and transport. Unless a corner can be given over to brambles, grow them under controlled conditions of pruning and training, otherwise they will soon take over. Should there be a corner to which brambles can be given unrestricted access, then I would suggest allowing nettles to proliferate there as well. Nettles provide breeding sites for several very handsome butterflies. In the nettle-grown copse alongside my own garden, red admiral, small tortoiseshell, comma, and peacock butterflies have all bred successfully over the last ten years. Considering the language used by blackberry pickers when confronted by the nettle-grown jungle I am surprised the caterpillars survive!

Once the plants are chosen and introduced then the basis of a community is established. A hedge, fence, or wall covered in vegetation becomes in effect a mini-woodland, offering shady or partially shaded areas, moist and cool with leaf litter. Only a yard or two away there is the open garden habitat stocked with plants chosen specifically as links in the chain. There will be no need to send out invitations to wildlife as I proved when sowing a lawn. Three days of hard labour were ruined in one night by a series of mole hills. My son's comment that I must have left some worms behind at least raised a smile.

SHRUBS

Berberis 'Barberry' A large genus made up of both deciduous and evergreen species. Deciduous 'Pirate King', 'Buccaneer' and all forms of aggregata. Prodigious masses of yellow flowers followed by long-lasting scarlet fruits. *B thunbergii* and varieties is indispensable. Evergreen *Berberis darwinii* is outstanding. *B stenophylla* makes a prime nest site much sought after by long-tailed tits – only for the larger garden though.

Buddleia 'Butterfly Bush' fast growing, quick lunch counters for a whole host of insects. as well as butterflies. *B alternifolia* 8 ft (2-3 m). Purple in June. A useful specimen weeping shrub. *B davidii* and hybrids – choose all or any of the various flower colours on offer.

Chaenomeles 'Quince' including *Cydonia oblonga* are useful in a modest way. Spiny, bushy, apple-like shrubs up to 10 ft (3 m). Flower colours range from white, pink, salmon, to scarlet. Fruit edible quince – ripe October – makes delicious jelly.

Clethra alnifolia (Sweet Pepper Bush) 7 ft (2 m). White flowers in September.

Cotoneaster In so large a genus there is something to suit every soil and situation. Range in height from ground cover like *humifusus (dammeri)* upwards. Flowers pink in bud open white. Berries red, yellow, orange.

Daphne Ornamental shrubs of modest size. *D mezereum* is best known 40 in (1 m). Purple flowers March followed by scarlet berries. *D retusa* is neatly evergreen – purple flowers white flowers. Red berries.

Mahonia Useful winter and early spring flowering evergreen shrubs. *M aquifolium* – ground cover, yellow flowers, blue-black edible berries. Forms of *M japonica* up to 7 ft (2 m). Yellow flowers February, blue-black berries July.

Pyracantha (Firethorn) Essential forage shrubs – insects eagerly scour the white flowers in June, birds the orange-red berries in late October. Height 2 ft to 11 ft (60 cm up to 3 m). Recommended 'Mojave', 'Orange Glow', 'Red Cushion' and 'Teton'.

Sambucus 'Elder' Forms of the native *S nigra* and naturalised *S racemosa* are excellent, quick establishing habitat plants. Height 6 ft plus (2 m). White flowers, red or black berries.

Viburnum Best serve the wildlife conscious gardener in the shape of *V lanata* 'Wayfaring Tree'. Height 10 ft (3 m). White flowers June, followed by red, then black berries. *V opulus* 'Guelder Rose' is the other native. Flowers white, berries red. *Compactum* should be the first choice for smaller gardens.

Bee keepers will need to plant Hazel (*Corylus*) and Willow (*Salix*) – they flower early and provide the bees, which venture out on sunny days, with protein rich pollen.

Heathers, which include all forms of *Calluna vulgaris* and *Erica* species are so obviously essential. Heathers make good groundcover. Wrens in particular haunt heathers and bees forage among them.

Some very beautiful native flowers grow naturally at hedge bottoms as I discovered when searching out the old drove roads and drift ways, which even today offer a respite from the tarmac and the 'infernal' combustion engine. Butterbur will spread from wet to open places; if you plant the species *Petasites fragrans* (winter heliotrope), you will be rewarded with vanilla scented flower spikes in February. *P hybridus* is the one most commonly seen along river banks. Coltsfoot, a near-relation of butterbur, will flourish in the drier, sun-warmed crannies to flower yellow in March. Wild *Arum* (known also as cuckoopint, and lords and ladies) is a strangely beautiful native plant with more than a hundred dialect names; its Latin title, *Arum maculatum*, can bring order to a chaotic selection of different names. Small midges are attracted to the flower by its colour and scent (of putrefying meat), and in their efforts to reach the closed cup succeed also in fertilizing the flowers, ensuring a full crop of ripe berries in due season. The berries are poisonous, yet birds eat them without ill-effect.

Bugle, white dead nettle, and hedge mustard together with ground ivy make good ground cover along a hedgeback and are much appreciated by insects. Hedge mustard, *Sisymbrium officinale*, is a favourite haunt of orange-tip and green-veined white butterflies.

Primroses mixed with wood violets are a feature in several of my spring haunts, so I copied this natural plant association to finish a corner of hedgeline. Primroses are selective in regard to soil and I ensure their well being with good drainage and lime: magnesium limestone chips worked into the soil prior to planting fulfil both requirements.

Meadow crane's-bill, giant bellflower and harebell were common hedgerow denizens along lane verges in the dale where I spent my childhood. Nostalgia apart, I would grow them anyway because they are beautiful and provide the heavy leaf cover and moist shade in which bird, beast, and amphibian can fruitfully forage and seek refuge. To hear a hedgehog rummaging beneath a well-furnished hedge is to be introduced to a whole new descriptive gourmet vocabulary. Toads and frogs require the undisturbed quiet furnished by the more overgrown, wild corners of the garden: such places afford protection and a larder ready-stocked with invertebrates of various sorts – their main food. Given suitable crevices, leaf or compost heaps in which to spend the winter, newts also will loiter year round in close proximity to a pond. These are provided naturally by a hedge or shrub-covered wall.

I was introduced to another aspect of habitat sharing only last week. The bird feeding ground includes the two compost bin lids, numerous hanging containers of peanuts and suet, plus the whole of a lawn 10 by 12 yards (about 10 by 12 metres) bounded by hedges on two sides, and a wall on the third. Mixed bird food is scattered on the lawn along with apple peelings and any rotten fruit I can harvest. That a fox enjoys a mixed diet of fruit and flesh I already knew as one visits the site most evenings. I was surprised one day when a piece of apple peeling suddenly shot off towards the hedge apparently of its own volition, then I noticed a mouse firmly attached to one end. Presumably, this was a wood mouse which, no doubt, made good use of

A mixed hedge will offer a wider variety of food and nesting or hiding places than a single species hedge. Underplant the shrubs and small trees with plants such as cuckoopint, primroses and wood violets.

the corn put out for the seed-eaters and was trying apple as dessert.

When mature a mixed hedge offers as diverse a habitat as many a monoculture woodland so planting even a short run with say, privet, hawthorn, blackthorn, wayfaring tree, holly, and elder would be a giant first step towards a wildlife composition. Allow wild rose, honeysuckle and ivy to share company with it and you present even better accommodation.

To witness the lifestyle of an ever increasing variety of wildlife at close quarters is one of the privileges to be enjoyed by anyone joining the hedge-planting fraternity. This morning I found a pheasant's nest alongside the holly section of the hedge bordering the east side of my garden. That the hen frightened me out of my wits as she took off is reason enough for me to avoid that corner for the next month.

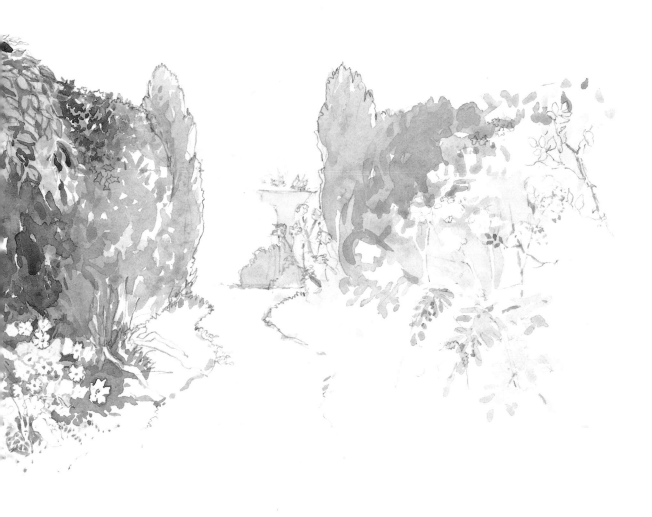

7. 'Meadows trim with daisies pied'

How to create the basis for your garden and a valuable food source for birds

Only ten years ago the fields surrounding my house were typical of pasture and meadow throughout the Dales. Now they have been reduced to a nitrogen-greened mediocrity. Cropped for silage twice a year, then plastered with slurry and tilled to force growth, they have in so short a time been transformed from meadowland into grass factories. Modern farming practice excludes all but the most adaptable wildflowers. I can compensate for this loss in a small way by growing the best of them in my garden. What will be impossible to replace is the richness of wildflower habitat which these same fields once offered.

There is not a vestige of life in what little is left of the small pond. Not a single lapwing overwintered on the fields last year from the hundreds which once foraged there and spring is the poorer for their absence. I miss their patterned, geometric tumbling and looping which has foretold spring all my life: the haunting lament of a lapwing's call is now part of old, remembered, far-off things. No corner of my lawn is remote or expansive enough to tempt lapwing or curlew to nest there, but I can enjoy watching thrushes heave worms out of unpolluted grass, and share company with yellowhammer, greenfinch and chaffinch which gather to harvest seedheads from grass and flowers.

Cultivators of wildlife gardens need to master the art of controlled neglect, for to allow a plot to tumble down to growing only plants indigenous to the area would, in fact, be self-defeating. Nowhere is this balance between natural and contrived so difficult to achieve as in that part of the garden designated to be made into lawn. Indeed, I have not yet reached a compromise in my own garden between lawn and meadow. Purists scoff at what is to them, my weed-infested lawn, while I am disappointed that professional gardening pride refuses to allow me to co-exist with a wildflower meadow so close to the house. Instead, I grow cowslip, meadow crane's-bill, ox-eye daisy, and snake's head fritillary in the flower borders.

By not using selective weed killers to reduce my lawn to grass only, plantains, dandelion, daisy, speedwell and other ground keepers survive. I cease mowing for a week or two in dry weather giving plants time to seed and my controlled neglect is rewarded with day's eyes of daisy, eye bright of speedwell, and the pollen-dusted drum sticks of plantain. A lawn untreated with chemicals usually supports a vigorous population of worms and other soil fauna which birds, shrews, and unfortunately, moles are not slow to investigate. In summer, leather jackets which have spent their formative years feeding on

This garden has a pleasant feel – the surrounding hedges and wall offer seclusion and shelter. The lawn is casual but fairly neat, a central place for children to play and birds to feed on.

'Meadows trim with daisies pied'

grass roots emerge in swarms as familiar daddy-long-legs or crane flies. Pied wagtails are equally aware of this annual event and hurry about the lawn like clockwork toys snatching the insects as they emerge. Starlings, those most conversational of birds, spend hours probing the turf for leather jackets, then fly off at intervals to offer thanks in a cascade of mimicry from the house roof. One starling humorist succeeded in copying my whistle so precisely, as to completely fool my dog, who eventually became quite disgruntled by the whole business of obedience. By separating ourselves from the world of animals we have impersonalised them. In a wildlife garden we can establish relationships with animals on a personal basis.

Laying down the sort of grassland which will grow wild flowers and an acceptable mixed sward of herbage requires a vastly different soil preparation to that recommended for an ornamental lawn. Those intent on achieving bowling green perfection will spare no effort or expense in working the soil to high fertility before sowing a seed or laying a turf. The idea is to have the grass growing so vigorously that it will compete successfully with any weeds seeking to gain a root hold. But in a rich soil only the coarser, less desirable, weed-like species flourish. A wildflower gardener therefore aims to reduce fertility to a level at which the greatest variety of species can co-exist. For an established lawn that is to be converted to mini-meadow, a programme of no feeding, combined with removing the mowings (instead of letting them fall back as a mulch), will reduce fertility in the space of a season. Time waiting can be profitably spent in raising cowslips, meadow crane's-bill, bugle, lady's-smock and sweet vernal grass from seed for 'plug' planting into the existing sward as opportunity arises.

Before beginning a pilgrimage in search of the ideal compromise between a lawn and meadow, there first has to be a decision on what particular goal we are endeavouring to reach. There is little point in searching for something when we have no clear idea of what the object of the quest looks like.

Until recently, grass fields used for grazing or cropping for hay were rarely ploughed. Gradually wild flowers colonised and adjusted to the routine cultivations used in the management of these comparatively undisturbed grasslands. Instead of one or two grass species, there were several including sweet vernal grass, upright brome, and the loveliest of all, quaking grass. By carefully examining the different grasses, it was possible, with practice, to make a fairly accurate assessment of soil type and the cultural history of the field.

Modern farming practice, even one application of fertilizer, wipes a page of farming history clean. Meadow and pasture flowers, which fortunately are still abundant in two fields near my home include ox-eye daisy, black knapweed, self heal, Lady's-smock, common mouse-ear and common spotted orchid. Buttercups, thistles and dandelions are also a feature in one or two over-grazed fields.

Watching small tortoiseshell butterflies feeding on spear thistle flowers, or the flickering brown shadow of a meadow brown butterfly busy about the pale lilac blooms of the pernicious, weed-like creeping thistle is enough to persuade of the benefits a less than perfect lawn can offer. Have a care in introducing some of the more weed-like meadow or pasture flowers into the garden, for once in, like some guests, they are hard to remove.

There is no minimum size for a wildflower meadow: a stretch of grass down a shrubbery edge, a patch near the compost heap or most aesthetically pleasing of all, a grassed-down orchard managed to benefit native flowers will all offer considerably more habitat than a smooth-mown lawn.

A field above my house which is mown for hay in July shows an entirely different floral pattern to the broad grass verge bordering the lane which is left uncut, ungrazed except casually by passing cows until blackberry picking time. In the hay field spring flowers flourish, particularly dandelion, cowslip, milkmaid and the like. On the lane verge which is really like a small field, meadow crane's-bill, lady's bedstraw, giant bellflower, buttercups, and purple vetch thrive.

The pattern of management for a mini-meadow will then depend on the sort of flowers planted in it. For a lawn in which spring flowering species predominate the herbage would need to be left uncut until mid June in the south, and early July in the north. This would give seed time to ripen and be shed by the hay-making process. Though in theory a mini-meadow might safely be mown in June, I find that favourites like the meadow crane's-bill are seriously inconvenienced if mowing extends much beyond about 10 May. The plot is then left uncut until late September, or if seed-eating birds are in evidence, October.

Last year I was standing on the edge of a newly established summer meadow which sloped down to a pool. The day was reluctantly giving way to twilight, and in the hushed quiet I was surprised at just how busy with life the area had become. Insects hummed, and there were rustlings and squeakings in the grass. Then, even as I was about to turn for home, a stoat emerged from the grass, stood on hind legs to survey the terrain, then undulated across the smooth-cut lawn to disappear into a dry stone wall. A small incident which added rather a special quality to the day.

Soil preparation before sowing the seed needs to be done with the same painstaking thoroughness as that required for a bowling green, except the accent is on seed bed preparation only and *not* on increasing the fertility by working in organic matter at the same time. Dig the soil over in autumn then leave it in rough clods for the frost to break down into an easily worked, friable state. After prolonged heavy rain, check to see if there are any areas where water collects and remains for long periods. Though permanently boggy areas can be used to advantage, patches which alternate between soggy wet and brick hard dry are of no value. Rather than suffer any inconvenience of this sort, make certain drainage is good over the whole site simply by laying a drain to a soak-away situated near the pond or wet place. In late March when the soil is dry enough, lightly fork the bed over, taking care to remove couch (twitch) grass roots and similar unwanted weeds. Another ground keeper, ground elder, if allowed to remain will soon swamp both meadow and garden.

Here I confess to being a committed autumn sower of lawns, so having cleaned the site I would plant early potatoes as these are off the land in time for the soil to be raked down into a seed bed for

Geoff Doré (Bruce Coleman Ltd)

sowing from mid August to early October whenever the weather permits. But with the land dug and seed bed preparation for an April sowing well in hand, then should the weather afford sunshine and showers to make soil steam like a kettle, snatch the opportunity offered and scatter the seed.

First rake the clods down to a fine tilth, roughly levelling the plot at the same time. Then firm the soil down by treading every part of it with your feet using what is known as the 'gardener's shuffle'. Feet are kept close together, with weight on heels, walking sideways as if the knees were tied together. When the whole area is well firmed, rake the soil down to an even level. Though the levelling need not be to a bowling green finish it still should be done thoroughly so as to remove hollows which hold moisture like mini-ponds after every shower.

Having advised on various measures aimed at reducing the fertility of the seed bed – a seeming contradiction – I always rake in a light dressing of superphosphate to encourage strong root development in the germinating seedling. At this stage offer a prayer for the dark green sunset that Virgil assures us stands for rain – not the flame colour foretelling an east wind for the seed once sown needs to grow quickly.

Much has been said and written over recent years since wildlife gardening became fashionable – advice on sowing first the grass, then 'plug' planting flowers into it. This works well and I always raise some cowslips, primroses, and especially orchids, in frames for planting once the ley is established. There is another method I have evolved since sowing my first meadow habitat for Alpine pasture plants some thirty years ago. For the first year's flowering I included some arable and cornfield weeds which, for one season at least, found

(Left) Cowslips can be 'plug-planted' into lawns with great success.

A great tit (right) suns itself in a patch on the edge of the lawn. The raised feathers and spread wings are typical of sunbathing birds.

A T Moffat (Aquila)

the conditions suited them admirably. Corn poppy (*Papaver rhoas*), cornflower (*Centaurea cyanus*), corn marigold (*Chrysanthemum segetum*), corncockle (*Agrostemma githago*) together with pansy (*Viola*) will, as John Clare insists, add 'a destroying beauty to your field'.

Gardeners on acid soil should also consider splitting the meadow into two, then dressing one section with lime, for the flowers found growing on alkaline soils are bewitchingly beautiful. The seeds I would sow direct, in addition to the arable sorts, include milkmaids (*Cardamine pratensis*) cat's ear (*Hypochoeris radicata*), hawkbit (*Leontodon*) and common mouse-ear (*Cerastium*) for the spring section. Daisy, dandelion and plantain will seed themselves in from roundabout. For summer, sow sheep's sorrel (*Rumex acetosella*) whose leaves I loved to nibble as a child for their mouth puckering, acrid flavour; knapweed (*Centaurea scabiosa*), ox-eye daisy (*Leucanthemum vulgare*), meadow crane's-bill (*Geranium*), and goat's beard (*Tragopogon pratensis*). At the same time, sow in a nursery bed or frame for 'plug' planting into the once or twice mown grass, cowslip (*Primula veris*), bugle (*Ajuga reptans*) along with self-heal (*Prunella vulgaris*), yarrow (*Achillea millefolium*), kidney vetch (*Anthyllis vulneraria*), bird's foot trefoil (*Lotus corniculatus*), devil's bit scabious (*Succisa pratensis*), field scabious (*Knautia arvensis*) and harebell (*Campanula rotundifolia*).

Some thistles are beautiful and useful hosts for insects: carline thistle (*Carlina vulgaris*), or the stemless thistle (*Cirsium acaulon*) which thrive on a lime soil are two. Of the numerous native orchids which I find so exceedingly fascinating, let me say that it is simpler to buy in plants and provide congenial conditions, than to hope they will naturalise.

I also find it sensible to buy bulbs for naturalising – autumn crocus (*Colchicum*), tulip (*Tulipa sylvestris*) our only native, and daffodils (*Narcissus pseudo-narcissus, and Narcissus obvallaris*), also snake's head fritillary (*Fritillaria meleagris*).

Living in a district where there are still what local farmers call 'old land meadows' cut for hay, I am able to make an economy on seed buying. In late winter I just ask a farmer friend for permission to sweep up the seed tailings from his haymow. The range of grasses, flowers, and other less welcome plants like docks and creeping thistle that come up after sowing the sackful of dust, wisps of hay and seeds is truly astonishing. That the farmer always makes the comment 'tha must be daft' in no way deters me. One day someone will tell him he is giving away a saleable by-product.

Selection of the grass seed which, in due course, will be sown to provide the basis of the habitat lawn-cum-meadow, other than scrounging the seed as I do, presents no problems. Seed merchants will provide a mixture to suit both soil and your requirements. Choosing which flowers to grow is very much a question of individual taste. Wildflower seeds, like the exotic garden varieties, are expensive, so be circumspect. Make out a select list of 'must haves' then another of 'nice to haves', and above all, buy from a specialist who stocks seeds collected from *native* plants.

There are three ways of introducing wild flowers into our lawn-cum-mini-meadow. The first is by mixing grass and flower seed together then sowing direct where they are to grow. The second is to sow the flower seed into frames or nursery beds, then when the young plants are large enough to cope with competition from the grass transplanting them into the grass sward. This I might add, in my experience, is the only route for those seeking to fashion a wildflower meadow out of a mature lawn. Method three, the one I use, is a compromise between the other two. I mark out small, irregular beds in the plot made ready to receive the grass seed and sow a pinch of the flower seeds into each, choosing from those I have already indicated as being suitable for direct sowing. The remainder of the seed I sow into frames or nursery beds where growing conditions can be more easily controlled than in the open garden. Watering a frame or small nursery bed is not laborious, and protecting the seed from birds easier than it would be elsewhere in the garden, so really what I am describing is a 'belt and braces' job. Having sown the irregular plots, broadcast the grass seed – allowing for a rate of 1½–2oz per square yard (42-57g per square m), and rake it in lightly.

Those of a nervous disposition might at this stage suffer less by going on holdiay for there is nothing more to be done until the seed starts growing. Watching birds eating, dust-bathing, and scratching like gold-crazed Klondyke miners in a bed prepared in brow beading, muscle straining effort, can reduce the strongest gardener to tears. A word of comfort to the beginner – experience teaches that enough seed usually survives to grow into a credible lawn.

Do not be surprised if the first indigenous mammal to test the hospitality offered announces his or her satisfaction by heaving up mounds of soil across the carefully graded surface. I cherish a certain sympathy for the mole that works with the same soil I labour over so assiduously; the only pity is our methods of going about the cultivation are totally at variance and are rarely complementary. Fortunately, what would spell disaster on a crown green bowling pitch is easily put right on a potential wild meadow. Just level the hills and if necessary re-seed the bare patches.

When the plot shows a thickening haze of green, roll it using the lightest implement available so as not to overcompact the soil. I find the lawn mower roller is ideal being heavy enough to flatten the lumps and break the grass shoots so as to make them 'tiller'. Then, instead of one shoot growing up, each seed will produce three or more to colonise the bare earth. A lawn sown in April or May should be cut with the mower set high at monthly intervals throughout the summer. The autumn sown lawn will need one or possibly more light toppings to settle the sward down before winter arrives.

One thing is certain, the mower used on the lawn proper will not be able to cope with long grass. Instead of buying a second machine which will be only used at most three times a year, just hire either a rotary, or reciprocating mower as necessary. After the first year, adjust the mowing so as to give the various flowers included in the cosmopolitan herbage the best possible conditions to grow, flower, ripen then shed seed to naturalise. Mow in June to early July for those which bloom in the spring, and September to early October for the summer flowering species.

Starlings like to feed on short grass. They probe the sward with dagger-like bills. Among their favourite grubs are leatherjackets.

8. 'All the trees that grow so fair, Oak and Ash and Thorn'

The trees and shrubs that you plant will last a lifetime

An avenue of beeches. With careful planting, trees will enhance both atmosphere and wildlife for many years.

The poet, taking a pinch of seed, exclaimed at holding a forest in his hand. Fanciful certainly, albeit true, and in the same way the shrub border or boskaged corner hiding the compost heap provides a valuable alternative so far as wildlife is concerned to the fast diminishing woodland.

Most of my childhood and teenage years were spent in an environment where farms, woodlands, and the countryside in general were managed on a pattern which had suffered little variation over decades. The woodlands were made up largely of native deciduous trees; beech, birch, ash, oak, underplanted with hazel, holly, and elder, with alders colonising stream edge and other wet places. Villagers insisted on the right of access handed down from generation to generation which enabled them to coppice hazel, ash, and other suitable trees capable of producing a fresh crop of shoots from stumps cut back to ground level. This simple method of coppicing undergrowth while allowing selected trees to grow and mature provided the diverse habitat which suited a broad selection of our native flora and fauna.

The coppice-with-standards system of woodland management provided almost precisely the same conditions for wildlife as a modern day mixed shrub border — or am I being too imaginative? For those childhood images of firewood collecting, primrose picking and nut gathering remain vivid in a bluebell-scented and leafmould fragrant memory. The seasonal progression of that wood is to a degree mirror-imaged in my own garden. Snowdrops and aconite opening in February under a silver birch grown from seed begin the pageant, closely followed by wood violets, primroses, anemones, bluebells, Solomon's seal, then herb Robert.

That gardens can offer roothold to these tenacious ancient Britons, direct descendants of the original wild woodlanders, is true beyond doubt and not merely whimsical fancy. Where flowers are, soon will appear butterflies and other insects which in turn attract birds, mice, hedgehogs and all the St Francis flock to share the food chain.

Who, when looking at an ancient oak tree growing on a copse edge, can fail to appreciate how important trees are in landscape and wildlife habitat terms. For such a tree has marked the passage of centuries and carries the scars of battle to prove it. From acorn to its eventual demise as a wind-blown stump, an oak tree provides food, shelter, and harbourage to an enormous range of plant and animal life. Not many gardens are large enough to accommodate a mature oak, though there are slow growing forms of both our native species which offer a useful alternative to the type. Taking a tree as a relative term, many can become imitation coppiced woodland, for shrubs put up shoots from ground level and some broad-leaved trees will stand hard pruning without becoming unsightly.

Prepare the soil so as to give the trees and shrubs you plant the best possible start. I dig the border over 20 inches (50 cm) deep, working in compost, rotted farm manure, leaf mould, or any other organic matter which will rot down and form humus fairly quickly. At this stage, check whether your soil contains lime if lime-intolerant shrubs like the common ling (*Calluna vulgaris*) are to form part of the association as, indeed, heathers do in the ancient Caledonian and Breckland Forests.

I prefer to grow shrubs and trees from seed when possible, finding the process immensely satisfying. I keep a frame and small nursery bed set aside for the purpose. Berries of hawthorn, holly, wild rose, rowan and the like need to be buried in pots filled with sand for a few months prior to sowing. As for the remainder, I sow those into pots filled with loam-based compost or direct into the nursery border.

Your tree, or trees if the garden is large enough, provide an upper canopy which chaffinch, tits, thrushes, jackdaws, and others of arboreal inclination will occupy. What trees you select will depend on the space available, personal preference, and to a limited extent only, the type of soil in which they will be planted.

Shrubs are the second phase in what might be called the stages of settlement, for the gardener works in reverse to the natural process of colonisation adopted by plants when a plot of earth is left uncultivated. First come the pioneers – broad-leaved weeds and grasses – equivalent to the gardener's annuals and herbaceous plants. Almost immediately, shrubs and trees seed themselves in to establish the three-tiered canopy capable of supporting the greatest variety of plant, animal and insect life. Left untended, after a slow progression of centuries, a balance or 'climatic climax' is established and maintained with only slight variations. What under natural conditions may take centuries, the gardener contrives in decades by reversing the process; trees first, then shrubs, followed by herbaceous plants, annuals and bulbs.

The three stages under natural conditions as they evolved would support a fairly clearly defined flora and fauna. Then as the multiple canopy developed, creating shaded corners, dry places, shelter, and increased fertility due to leaf litter, so then would bird, beast, and creepy-crawly move in to exploit them. There is no waiting on the slow passing of centuries for the wildlife to move into the garden 'pseudo-woodland'. I only need threaten the soil with a fork or spade and there is a robin, head poised in enquiry, under my feet. Within months of planting up the borders birds had established territories. A blackbird in the holly bush, the first of a succession of blue tits discovered the holes left in the garage wall within ten days, even though I planted *Pyracantha* to mask them. Of course, the dunnock soon made use of the newly installed yard (metre) high beech hedge, while bees foraged busily about the crocus flowers brought from my previous garden and pushed into a corner near the compost heap as a temporary home.

SMALL TREES

Amelanchier (Snowy Mespilus) 20 ft (6 m). Racemes of white flowers April – black berries June. Grows best in moist, acid soil.

Betula (Birch) 10 ft (4 m) – 50 ft (15 m). Quick-growing, attractive barked, deciduous trees.

Cotoneaster Tall growing forms include *Cornubia* 18 ft (5 m), *Frigida* 20 ft (6 m). Both have white flowers followed by red berries.

Cotoneaster hybridus 'Pendulus' Up to 11 ft (3 m). Pink flowers, red berries. Best where space is limited.

Crataegus (Hawthorn) Tough, hardy, useful in flower and fruit. Form easily managed small trees as they are tolerant of hard pruning.

Ilex (Holly) Particularly the native species and varieties, is essential. Holly provides shelter, secure nest sites, flowers and berries. Unfortunately, male and female flowers are carried on separate plants, so do make sure both sexes are included.

Trees are the upper canopy of a garden. Those with holes provide nesting sites for many birds, including jackdaws.

Malus (Crab apple) Lightly branched trees of moderate size. Free-flowering and fruiting so a must in habitat and ornamental terms. 'Golden Hornet', 'John Downie', and 'Red Sentinel' are useful varieties. *M floribunda* and *sieboldii* are choice species.

Prunus (Cherry) There are so many to choose from for this is a large genus. *P avium* and *padus*, the Gean and Bird Cherry, being native are obviously worthy of consideration. *P sargentii* is very ornamental and bullfinches leave the buds intact.

Prunus laurocerasus Cherry laurel forms useful shelter and nesting site. White flowers, then black berries. *P lusitanica* is the more attractive. I grow the narrow-leaved *P laurocerasus* 'Schipkaensis' which is very free-flowering. Apart from these, choose any Cherry which fancy dictates and the garden can support.

Pyrus (Pear) Useful, early flowering, insect forage plants. *P salicifolia* 'Pendula' 14 ft (4 m) high. White flowers, grey leaves.

Sorbus (Rowan – Whitebeam) Prime wildlife plants in flower and fruit. *Sorbus x hosta, S aucuparia* 'Fastigiasa'. Both no more than 14 ft (4 m) high in maturity, suitable where space is limited.

Having decided where to plant your trees, perhaps using an umbrella as a marker, prepare the ground. Planting is best carried out during the tree's dormant period (autumn-spring) unless the plant is container grown. Make sure the hole is both wide and deep enough to accommodate the root ball easily. Then loosen the soil below for another six inches (15 cms). Add some rotted manure, compost or bone meal. Support the tree with a stake and bands (wire or string are not suitable), and protect if necessary against damage by rabbits or livestock. Water young trees frequently and keep a clear patch of soil around them until they are well established.

So, almost as the shed door closed shut signalling the end of my first day's work, the garden became a habitat – not theirs and mine – just ours. One observation I made during the first few weeks: rabbits will feed on road verges in preference to fields dressed with high nitrogen fertilizer. That those same rabbits discovered and exploited the fact that I am an organic gardener soon became obvious, and all new plantings had to be protected with sleeves or netting.

A mistake it is to confine the planting to only indigenous British flora when the native fauna show a more catholic taste, sipping nectar from a Chinese *Buddleia* with the same alacrity as when feeding on a native guelder rose.

The system I adopt once the major features have been decided on and located in the garden is simple and practical. Trees and shrubs are the focal points, each one is made the nucleus around which I build a plant community. What I am doing in practice is treating the garden as a series of small units, each one complete in landscape and habitat terms. This is much less daunting than trying to carry out a grand design of the whole garden and allows a greater degree of flexibility. Each member of the group is selected for a particular purpose. Possibly the system is easier to understand if I give an example.

Phase one is the centre piece of the mini-design, in this case a crab apple grown from seed. In 12 years, the pip has grown into a specimen 10 feet (3 metres) high; in flower, fruit, and habitat requirements this tree serves very well. The broad-leaved *Hosta fortunei* 'Glauca', I confess, was chosen more for aesthetic than practical reasons. Then the first generation of froglets showed their approval when they migrated from the pond by the shortest possible route, to the first available cover which was under the dense canopy of *Hosta* leaves. What is interesting about this mass migration of young frogs, is that they all leave the pond virtually on the same day.

Two parts of the community installed and functioning made an encouraging beginning. A shrub layer was the next and possibly most important consideration. Once again the seed pan provided a suitable candidate in the shape of the common azalea (*Rhododendron luteum*) which grew 4 feet (1·2 metres) high in ten years. The flowers carried in a rounded head are rich yellow in colour and have a most pleasing fragrance. Pollinating insects are attracted to this shrub in swarms for it is a hungry gap filler. The autumn colour of the leaves is a picturesque combination of red and gold which does nothing for the wildlife but delights me. There is a holly included in the design for in winter the bed of deciduous shrubs lacked character and supplied little or no protection. I chose the best berry-bearing female from those holly trees already growing in the shade border. I am never reluctant to move shrubs or trees from one part of the garden to another. Given a little care, even specimens 10 feet (3 metres) high will transplant without realising they have been moved. Then to form a link between this group and the one next to it, I planted a *Mahonia japonica*. This is a lovely shrub, worth growing for the beauty of its lustrous evergreen foliage, then excellence becomes perfection when the racemes of fragrant yellow flowers open in March just when insect food is scarce and I need the solace of flowers to cure the malaise left by the east wind of winter. The berries which ripen in July-

The Joy of Wildlife Gardening

August are the colour of black grapes, if you get a glimpse of them vanishing down some backbird's throat. Ground cover is made up with winter aconites, bluebells, crocuses, and primroses. Followed in summer by a curious 'Billy Button', *Geum*, and *Achillea* 'Galaxy', with Michaelmas daisy as a final accolade in autumn. Now with the three tier system well established the group looks attractive and offers shelter and food which I supplement with an insect harbouring mulch.

The temptation to reproduce in the garden one of the many attractive wildlife habitats which are still to be found is, at times, irresistible. Commonsense and the limitations imposed by lack of space have so far stopped me attempting the impossible task of trying to reproduce a Teesdale scar or Devon combe in a border 50 by 10 yards (46 by 9 metres). What *is* possible, given a spirit of compromise, is to take the grand landscape as a pattern and scale it down to fit the space available. With so many plant permutations to work with, this scheme is not so fanciful as it sounds.

Rowan, *Sorbus aucuparia*, that near-indestructible relative of the wild service tree, and whitebeam look magnificent growing amongst silver birch along the borders of a stream. In the small garden a tree 30 to 40 feet (10 to 13 metres) high in maturity becomes with the passage of years a liability, so *Sorbus* are overlooked in favour of something smaller. Then I found that the dwarf rowan, *Sorbus aucuparia* 'Fastigiata' looks and behaves like the full blown species, opening clusters of white blossom in May that form bunches of red berries by August, so I planted that instead. In 11 years, this slim-fit rowan has grown into a handsome specimen with a crown measuring 12 ft 7 inches high (3·2 metres) by 52 inches (1·3 metres) across. The flowers are insect-pollinated, which probably explains why the whitethroat, which nests in or near the copse each spring, spends so much time perched on this particular tree. Blackbirds have already polished off the berries before the first wave of fieldfares crosses the coast: they usually perch after feeding on an apple tree near the well for purposes of rumination, digestion, and judging by the number of seedlings which spring up, toiletry as well.

Willows are usually represented in gardens by the weeping *Salix chrysocoma* which takes up an inordinate amount of the available space. Again, there are dwarf willows which, while not so grandly expressive, do perform the dual ornamental habitat function. The Kilmarnock willow, *Salix caprea* 'Pendula' forms a most attractive mushroom headed, stiffly pendulous tree up to 9 feet (3 metres) high. The naked branches are set with pearl grey catkins which are a useful food source to insects just out of hibernation. One moth which I have not succeeded in identifying rewards the tree for hospitality rendered by laying eggs which hatch into caterpillars which then strip all the foliage. Though blue tits account for a good number there are enough left to reduce the wretched tree to indecent mid-summer nakedness. I also grow the woolly willow, *Salix lanata*, a rare native growing only a metre or so high. The silver-grey downy leaves suffer no damage from caterpillars, and the large pollen-dusted catkins are visited by pollen seeking insects.

I grow sweet gale, both male and female, close by. They have

A few trees and a well sited nestbox might tempt blue tits to breed in your garden rather than just visiting it for the winter. Oak trees provide them with plenty of caterpillars for their nestlings in the early months of the year.

golden brown catkins which glisten as if varnished, and the whole plant gives off a strong, resinous scent. There is a reddish brown, yellow-striped caterpillar which feeds on the foliage of gale myrtle in the wild, though I have not seen it yet on plants in gardens.

Our native holly is one of the most ornamental of evergreens and one of the top ten shrubs in the wildlife conservation list. To date I have 14 different varieties growing in my garden, 80 per cent have variegated leaves, the remainder self-sown from bird delivered seed are the plain-leaved species *Ilex aquifolium*. As a nest site for birds holly has few equals. When the berries ripen the native fruit eaters have to compete with fieldfares, redwings, and on occasion rodents for a share of the scarlet bounty. Apart from all this, were our native holly ugly as a mill chimney there would still be a corner of the garden reserved for this evergreen, for without it there would be fewer holly blue butterflies. Not that *Ilex aquifolium* is the only host for this flickering bye-blow of spring for ivy and buckthorn are also called upon to serve as nurseries. This is why the wall behind one of the largest of the holly bushes is planted with three forms of ivy, another of my top ten habitats.

In the hedge made up of hawthorn, holly, beech, and elder I have just planted blackthorn which blossoms early, ripens bitter sloe fruit late, and whose dense tangle of thorn armed twigs make them a much sought after nest site. Chaffinches and greenfinches along with dunnock prefer blackthorn and, of course hawthorn, to almost any other for nesting purposes. One day if fortune smiles, the lovely black hairstreak might join the holly blue butterfly and lay eggs on the newly planted blackthorn.

Hawthorn (*Crataegus*), holly (*Ilex*) and ivy (*Hedera*), three of the top ten, plus blackthorn (*Prunus spinosa*) make a habitat composition of native plants that would be hard to better in wildlife terms. I have added a bush of cherry plum (*Prunus cerasifera*) as a flanker, for my wife makes a most delicious pie with the fruit.

The orange-tip is one of the first butterflies to appear from eggs laid on hedge mustard which grows along the hedge bordering the copse. *Cotoneaster* is, if my observations are correct, a favourite feeding ground for this graceful butterfly which, like daffodils, 'often come before the swallows dare'. I discovered this by accident, for *Cotoneaster* is another of the top ten bird attractors, first to insects which cluster on the open flowers, then to the berries which ripen just as the last rowan berry is harvested. So often the value of flowers is overlooked by the more binocular-visioned ornithologist. The *Cotoneaster* is in bloom just when the migratory birds arrive, spent and needing a readily accessible supply of insects. *Cotoneaster hybridus* 'Pendulus' makes a neat, weeping bush some six feet (two metres) high, profuse in flower and prodigal in berry.

Cotoneaster horizontalis in flower, berry, and autumn colour is so ornamental and useful as to be nigh indispensable. I grow several including the variegated form against walls where the fan shaped branches afford made-to-measure nest-sites. Last year a 'Jennie wren' raised a brood of diminutive, hot-tempered termagants in the specimen growing on the garage wall. However, all cotoneasters are food providers in one form or another so are good ground rent payers.

Robert Gillmor

Delicate little birds, long-tailed tits feed on the seeds of alder and birch trees.

The Joy of Wildlife Gardening

Plants of the genus *Berberis* improve on the *cotoneaster* in being more secure as nesting sites, for the barrier of thorns is proof against the most venturesome predators, namely cats and small boys. Include the evergreen species *B. darwinii* (as I have mentioned previously, it is excellent), though the berries are stripped from every twig before summer's end. Extend the season with varieties of *B. aggregata*, and *B. thunbergii* whose branches hang berry-laden until January, at least in my garden, before being set upon by the birds.

Roses are first-class ornamental shrubs, only third rate hosts to wildlife if one excludes sawfly, aphids, leaf-cutter bees, and thrip. Though the hybrids are of limited worth, *Rosa rubrifolia*, *R. rugosa*, and other species with single or semi-double flowers carry their hip fruit into autumn and are good value. Some of the most vivid wildlife cameos of my experience concern roses. Foxes eating dog rose hips early one hoar-frosted morning is one. Watching a near gold coloured wood mouse foraging for hips on a hedge of 'Penzance briars' in bright harvest moonlight is another. That I was trying to teach a tawny owl raised from a downy chick to forage for itself instead of eating butcher's meat wrapped in chicken feathers, is another story. Interesting that the hips on the roses growing in laneside hedgerows in the dale are not eaten until the new year.

Do not let the word native, especially in regard to trees, persuade you into planting trees which are, in my experience, fit only to be grown in woodland or copse. Two of the worst offenders are ash, a true native, and sycamore, an introduced genus gone feral: they are a singularly unprincipled pair, seeking by self-sown seedlings to spread their multitudinous offspring far and wide. Though our native birch is too large for small wild gardens, the form listed as 'Youngs weeping birch' (*Betula pendula* 'Youngii') is small, mushroom-headed and modestly ornamental. The long-tailed tits, most appealing of the clan, show a distinct partiality for birches as well stocked winter larders, so there is the best possible excuse to plant one.

I also grow an upright hornbeam, the word upright makes a very graceful tree sound like an ecclesiastical teetotaller. However, *Carpinus betula* 'Fastigiata' grows commendably upright so shrubs can be grouped close to it. I grew a very neat, compact evergreen *Berberis candidula*, and the *Buddleia* 'Lochinch' as part of the shrub community associated with hornbeam. A word here of praise for all forms of *Buddleia davidii*, they are well named the 'butterfly bush'. 'Lochinch', with *B. davidii* as one parent and *B. fallowiana* as the other, makes a bushy, compact, grey-leaved shrub with dense conical spikes of very fragrant, violet-blue, orange-eyed flowers appearing in August. Butterflies fight for a turn at imbibing the juices distilled by the florets. There is another *Buddleia* introduced 25 years later than *davidii* called *alternifolia* which is totally different in character and flowers in June. Grown as a standard it makes an excellent 'tree' for the small garden, lovely when the pendulous branches are wreathed with lilac flowers whose scent reminds me of sun-warmed violets. Butterflies, bees, and a vast range of other nectar and pollen addicts add, an at times strident undertone to a June day in the garden.

Hawthorn, abundantly evident as it is in the hedgerows, might be considered sufficiently plentiful without including it in our garden

The orange-tip butterfly (only the male has orange-tipped wings) lays its eggs singly – the caterpillars are cannibals.

scheme. A compromise can be arrived at by planting forms of 'May', *Crataegus monogyna*, and the less common though still native *C. oxyacantha* to serve as a dual purpose decoration and wildlife pantry. In flower, then in autumn as the haws colour scarlet to match the dying leaves, the thorn is a handsome sight. There are less problems than with some trees keeping either species or varieties in order, for all of them stand hard pruning with enviable unconcern. Hedges of thorn form boundaries to the fields all about the dales here and at all seasons they are thriving, populous places. Birds build their nests in them and find secure roosting sites amongst the tangle of thorny branches. The young leaf buds are eaten by some birds, small children and, I suspect, some rodents. There are several score of insects if not dependent upon, at least associated with, hawthorn at various seasons. Included amongst them the hawthorn sawfly which look like chubby, fast-flying bumble bees crossed with a bluebottle. Their larvae are a food source for the tits and other birds that also search out the oval brown cocoons of the hibernating stage which are common sight on hawthorn twigs during winter. One of the eagerly awaited events of the autumn is the arrival of great flocks of fieldfares and redwings to feast on the berry laden bushes, so all in all the hawthorn is, together with the oak, a most important contributor to the wild, or if in the garden, half-tame wildlife larder. In my recollection, 'May' blossom and the tinkling, melodious call of the warblers are closely associated, an essential cogenitor of spring.

There are native cherries of particular interest to the wildlife gardener in that they add beauty to the landscape and sustenance to the local fauna. *Prunus avium*, the wild cherry or gean, is one of our most attractive native trees: in spring as the clusters of white flowers open with the green of bursting bud, then again in the autumn when the foliage turns crimson. Small, shiny fruit which succeed the flower are eaten, from my observations, by every creature furred or feathered who can gain access to them. *Prunus padus* or 'bird cherry', is well named, for its fruits are to blackbirds what green figs are to me; utterly irresistible! Being more a shrub than a tree means the scent of vanilla distilled by the drooping racemes of white flowers is nearer to any nose that happens to come within sniffing range. The black fruits are, of course, devoured as they ripen, even though they are very bitter to my taste. In my youth, the woods near my home were bordered by bird cherries and a variety of wildlife took full advantage of this freely available bounty. The scent of bird cherry flowers and the May choristry of the nightingale provided one of my unforgettable experiences – so my regard for the tree is not without bias.

Crab apples grow in almost every one of the hedges bordering the five lanes leading off from the village below my house. I grow five trees in the garden. All of them seedlings grown from hips, they are now nine years old. Four flower and fruit well, while the fifth is in quantity of flower and small amber coloured apples the most prolific of its kind in my experience. To see blackbirds straining, as they do each year, to swallow the apples whole gives a new meaning to the term 'honest endeavour'. The best time of all is in late May when the blossom laden branches are conversational with pollinating insects, and in July when the small ermine moth is abroad. To germinate the

The holly blue butterfly lays its first batch of eggs on holly leaves; the second brood of butterflies lays its eggs on the flower buds of ivy.

The Joy of Wildlife Gardening

apple pips I just sow them as I do all tree seeds – in clay pots filled with loam based compost then stand them in a cold frame.

I have a fondness for alder (*Alnus glutinosa*) which, when used in the right context, really is a very attractive native tree. The association goes right back to childhood when my father, after being persuaded to cycle with me the two miles to Ghyll Beck, identified the birds feeding on the alder seeds as siskins, until then creatures existing only in the pages of my Wayside and Woodland Series, *Book of British Birds*. That a vast number of insects are associated with alder makes this a useful tree for planting in a wet place if such a one exists or can be contrived. Plants such as the marsh marigold, yellow flag iris, and pendulous sedge grow well in association with alder. I know of one location where redpolls gather regularly each year in a remote valley high up on the moors to practise their extraordinary acrobatics in search of alder seed. Given also a nearby pond for the larvae to live in, and providing there is a sufficient accumulation of mud in the bottom, alder flies will soon be in evidence. I cannot faithfully promise that alder moth will also appear, having only once seen this dark brown and grey-fawn moth's black and yellow caterpillars feeding on alder. A useful grouping around a wet place is contrived with sweet gale (*Myrica gale*), *Salix gracilistyla* with handsome grey, red, then yellow catkins, and golden elder (*Sambucus nigra Aurea*), or *Viburnum opulus* 'Compactum' on the drier slopes.

To quicken the formation of a typical woodland soil I use a variety of mulches which range from rotted compost or manure to anyone of several grades of forest bark. To understand the sort of conditions you are striving to achieve, spend a day looking in hedge bottoms, copses, and mature woodland. There will be material in all stages of being broken down by insects, bacteria, and fungi from quite large branches to small leaves. That you will find such a study introduces you to a whole range of hitherto hidden gnawers, chewers, and munchers will be additional excuse for what some might call time wasting. Decaying, woody material left around the garden will soon be invaded by fungi of various sorts which will declare an interest by producing the familiar toadstool fruiting bodies. The less welcome stinkhorn fungus advertises its presence with the penetrating odour of rotting meat which blow flies find irresistible. Slugs, snails, certain rodents and, I suspect, other animals, particularly foxes, eat toadstools.

Keep a watch for the golden yellow and brown caps of honey fungus which is sometimes called 'bootlace' from the black, string-like underground 'roots'. This most adaptable fungus can live on dead organic matter where it, of course, performs a useful function, then from that secure base attack live, apparently healthy trees and shrubs. Cleanliness and strict garden hygiene provide no safeguard against attack by honey fungus. A stake used to support a pillar rose can just as easily give a home for honey fungus to attack from as a decaying branch left lying for black stag's horn beetles and woodlice to use as a nursery.

Just thinking of one unit in the woodland, copse edge, or coppice habitat we are endeavouring to simulate calls to mind many more reasons for leaving things natural. Slugs congregate under wood as the hedgehog family here soon discovered and benefited from.

Trees and shrubs (clockwise from top): hornbeam, hawthorn, alder, crab apple, elder, *Berberis*, gean, golden weeping birch.

Indeed, it was while watching two of the youngsters rooting under wood litter in the copse that I saw the peculiar self-anointing habit practised by hedgehogs. What purpose covering their spines in spittle froth serves I have yet not discovered.

When wood is scarce I put down straw bales which offer the same cool, moist seclusion to slugs, worms, and the wrens detected before I did a never failing insect larder. One year when I lifted a half decayed bale for composting, there amongst a stampede of crawlers were two smooth newts taking a holiday from life in the pool.

The complex pattern of inter-dependent life built up in the countryside over centuries of uninterrupted progress relies for its well-being on each individual part continuing to function intact. By studying even a small, undisturbed natural habitat you can build up an almost exact replica on a smaller scale in the garden. Disguise the straw bale, log heap, and stick pile with clumps of foxgloves (one of the 'must-have' flowers) and also white and red deadnettle, the deliciously fragrant woodruff, and even the trailing stems of honeysuckle, old man's beard (*Clematis vitalba*), and, if there is light enough, red campion.

Once all the integral parts are included the free loaders soon move in so that work becomes relegated to second place to the business of just watching, with ever increasing interest, how many birds, beasts, and insects are dependent on the facilities provided. Make notes of things which are to you unusual even though they are common knowledge in scientific circles. Items noted like: 'red damselfly established territory beside greenhouse steps', or 'Long-tailed tits seem able to converse and feed on birch seeds at one and the same time' are marvellous memory stimulators. Occasionally such committed watchers discover some hitherto unknown fact.

After all, the apple could have fallen on your head instead of Newton's!

Willow warbler on honeysuckle.

9. Those lazy, hazy days

Gradually the pattern of life about the garden changes. There is no slackening of tempo, rather a switch of emphasis. Instead of spending hours advertising his prowess as a lover from the cherry tree, the blackbird is proving his capability as a father by heaving worms out of the lawn to feed new-fledged nestlings. Pipistrelle bats hawk low over the pond in the short hours of twilight and lesser darkness when the space is vacated by the house martins and swallows.

In the flower and shrub borders the youthful promise of spring has matured by almost imperceptible degrees into the loveliness of high summer. Delphiniums hold court and communion with roses across lawns showing signs of discomfort under the burning heat of noon. Astonishing, that hot though the weather is, house martins can still find energy to hawk for the abundant insects needed to feed a brood rapidly growing too large for the nest tucked close under the eaves.

A spotted flycatcher built a nest on the limestone wall near the barn every summer during the seemingly interminable years of my childhood, the cobweb and lichen structure blending so perfectly with the masonry as to be almost invisible. The flycatcher's pursuit of insects is like some delicately executed aerial ballet, compared with the high-powered, incisive hawking of the swifts.

A toad took up residence each year beside the water tank inside the greenhouse. Once the annual procreative passion had expended itself in one brief outburst, life at least for this particular toad became a leisurely process of feeding, sleeping and being splashed with water as cans were filled from the tank.

As the fruit ripens on gooseberries, raspberries, and the mouth-watering, succulent strawberries, so bird, beast, and human animal vie with each other for a share. Chief plunderers of the strawberry bed are the blackbirds. My first task as a trainee gardener each morning during the fruit season, was to make sure no birds were trapped in the cotton netting used to cover soft and wall fruits. I sometimes wonder at the wisdom of the choice, for a fruit-hungry teenager consumed more strawberries, or 'White Heart' cherries than a whole bevy of blackbirds. Avian interest is not entirely confined to effecting access to ripening fruit; for some birds, peas offer a most acceptable alternative. In my first garden 'Irish peach' apples were the earliest to ripen. This is one apple which must be eaten fresh picked from the tree or the flesh turns to cotton wool, so for birds and children there was a brief time of plenty.

Draining of pools, combined with dredging of river beds has reduced once thriving waterside populations of plant and animal life

G D Smith

to an alarming degree. So with the loss of natural wetlands, the garden pool and its surroundings has gained an ever increasing importance as an alternative wetland, community centre. Dragonflies, those brightly coloured creatures of the sun, spend the summer days hunting their prey over the lily-studded waters of ponds and streams. Along with the more slender and finely wrought damselflies, they offer an irresistible excuse to lean on a hoe in contemplation. Indeed, the dragonfly in particular is the insect counterpart of the falcon, in that it captures prey on the wing. When poised, the forelegs of a dragonfly form a basket which it uses to capture airborne prey. Whether darters which fly out from a convenient perch to seize their noon-time snack, or hawkers which cruise around in search of succulent morsels, dragonflies offer abundant interest to the waterside watcher. Yellow flag iris, purple loosestrife, meadow sweet numerous with insect life are a profitable hunting ground to dragonflies, swallows, and house martins during the day and bats during the evening.

Only when August throws wispy veils of mist over the garden should the conservation orientated gardener begin hedge trimming. By then even the second brood of young birds will have left the nest. I am always surprised by the hitherto unsuspected number of nests hedge clipping reveals. How, for example, did a dunnock manage to build a nest and feed a brood of youngsters in the beech hedge down one side of the herb garden without my noticing? The thrush's nest I had watched almost from when the birds began a discussion as to where the best location would be. Once I intervened with a well aimed clod of earth when a neighbour's cat threatened one of the young birds resting on the lawn after a flying lesson, so my clipping of the hedge only revealed details of a familiar structure.

A little group of *Buddleia* 'Lochinch' planted in a corner sheltered from the wind by the beech hedge attracts a mixed collection of

(Above) Summer flowers – delphiniums, candytuft and foam of the meadow against a background of Young's weeping birch, Japanese maple and weigela.

(Right) Look out for bats on warm, summer evenings, when they will come to hunt insects around night-scented flowers and shrubs. This is a long-eared bat, a common species. You can encourage bats by putting up a bat box – made rather like a nestbox for a blue tit, but with a narrow entrance slot (about a finger's width) running underneath.

insects. In between bouts of nectar sipping, peacock, painted lady, and wall brown are amongst the good number of butterflies which sun themselves on the hedge. Sedums, golden rod, and the groups of late-sown annuals such as 'foam of the meadow', and *Phacelia* provide an alternative snack bar to the *Buddleia*. Sowing groups of annual flower seed about the garden in June to provide welcome colour, and producing insect food as a by-product in late summer, was a practice I adopted when keeping bees.

Groups of common ling (*Calluna vulgaris*) are colourful, labour-saving garden plants and useful dwarf shrubs for foraging insects. Slow worms and grass snakes soon discover a heather bank broken by drystone retaining walls give most acceptable accommodation. The bare patches between the groups of heathers or the sun-warmed stones are ideal spots for a snake to take siesta, with the unmortared recess in the wall a safe retreat. My first encounter with a grass snake was on just such a heather bank sloping down to a stream. I was supposed to be hard at work top-dressing bare soil with leaf mould when my attention was drawn to what looked like an outsized eel swimming across the tadpole-filled pool. Only when the supposed eel wriggled out onto the bank, coiled like a carelessly dropped piece of rope on the rough hewn stone path did I realise that it was, in fact, a grass snake. A dip in the pool, combined with a light lunch of tadpoles, followed by a luxurious sun bath, proved to me (a son of toil), that the snake fared better than Adam in the dispute of Eden.

The vegetable garden and orchard are an open air harvest festival as the spring's fruits of labour mature. Though the cabbage white butterflies are a familiar part of the summer scene, in practice their presence indicates that a careful inspection of the Brussels sprouts, cauliflowers, and cabbages would not go amiss. Hand-picking of caterpillars is a most effective control of this particularly unwelcome visitor. The only time I ever enjoyed a near caterpillar free garden was when two Siamese cats shared it with me. They spent hours catching butterflies, lurking in the cool shade of rows of brassicas to leap out on any unsuspecting butterfly which dared venture too near in search of a prospective caterpillar dormitory.

There should always be a seat conveniently near the herb garden, for it was just such a seat which introduced me to the pleasure of herb-sniffing. The sprinkler having been busy moistening the sun-baked lawn, the herb garden was thoroughly soaked in the process. In early evening I was detailed to move the sprinkler to another part of the vegetable garden, and having completed this small yet essential task, the seat offered an irresistible temptation to leisurely enjoyment of a warm summer evening. The combined odour of moist grass and the bouquet garni from the herbs persuaded me to a habit I have indulged in many times since.

Summer then is a pod of green peas picked and eaten straight from the bine; discovering apples gathered with the damp, coolness of night adding to the sweet succulent juiciness to make a most refreshing pre-breakfast snack; or is it just the season when being outdoors is preferable to even the most comfortable seat indoors, offering as it does a more intimate acquaintance with the abundant, teeming life of the garden?

Kim Taylor

69

C H Gomersall (RSPB)

10. 'Daffodils that come before the swallows dare'

Bring colour to your garden to feast your eyes and feed a host of insects

Once the basic design of a garden is established with trees and shrubs and herbaceous borders as the permanent framework, there is a need for seasonal change. I agree the plants listed do measure the seasons, the same year after year with only minor variations, and therein lie the seeds of boredom. By a judicious use of bulbs and annuals the whole character of a garden can be changed to provide seasonal variety.

Many bulbs are, of course, perennial. Drifts of daffodils colonies of crocus, themes of tulips, and leagues of lilies will, given scope, spread into even larger groups. Yet they are a form of instant garden in that most of them flower a few months after being planted. Only when I began to take an interest in bee-keeping did the importance of bulbs as a forage plant become obvious. Prior to my acquisition of five hives and three colonies of bees, bulbs were just an essential part of garden decoration. I also thought that bees were sensible creatures that hibernated from November to April – a commendable habit shared by most insects, bugs, and beetles to avoid the inclemency of winter. Then one warm day in February while admiring a drift of *Crocus tomasinianus* 'Whitwell Purple' I noticed the flowers were being busily worked by hordes of bees. That they were non-gardening neighbour's bees taking advantage of flowers growing in my garden sent me hot foot to open the slides on my own hives. To this day I am convinced I heard one of the bees say 'about time too' as it hurried past me.

For naturalising there is no crocus more efficient at covering naked earth with self-sown offspring than *Crocus tomasinianus*. The lilac coloured flowers intermingle with snowdrops and aconite to form a shadow of lilac, white and yellow under the *Mahonia japonica* in this garden. To follow on from *C. tomasinianus*, the various forms of *Crocus chrysanthus* in all shapes, sizes and variety are graceful, delightful garden decoration and useful forage plants for bees.

Snowdrops, once established, soon settle into an ever-expanding colony. I prefer to plant the bulbs in growth, having experienced some difficulty in persuading dry bulbs to settle in. Snowdrops prefer old, damp woodland type soil, so I offer them the best simulation. While the oak tree which I am growing from an acorn busily attains a respectable size, the woodland consists of hazel underplanted with snowdrops.

Winter aconites (*Eranthis hyemalis*), one of the earliest flowers to appear in the year, are also best transplanted in growth. I set the dried corms in pots or boxes filled with equal parts of leaf mould and loam, let them grow and flower, then plant the corms while still in leaf into

Daffodils naturalised in a lawn are one of the simplest pleasures of spring. Plant them in clumps, replacing the plugs of turf, in areas which will not need to be mown until early summer.

The snake's head fritillary (*Fritillaria meleagris*) – one of my favourite plants.

the garden. Include also a hosting of bluebells to add that joyously fragrant, essential ingredient of the woodland in spring.

A few roots of moschatel, *Adoxa*, the 'town hall clock' of childhood, so named because the head of flowers are arranged like four clock faces around the stem, can be planted with the bluebells.

Daffodils 'that come before the swallow dares and take the winds of March with beauty', hold all the gentle, fragile loveliness of spring in the yellow-petalled flowers. In respect of the whole clan *Narcissus*, I adhere closely to species or near species, finding them easier to establish and more expressive of the informality which I find so essential, than the large, more extravagantly coloured hybrids. *Narcissus pseudo-narcissus* is a native and needs a moisture-retentive soil to thrive. *Narcissus poeticus*, 'Pheasants Eye', is always associated in my memory with unsprayed meadowlands which were filled more with wild flowers than grass. In gardens the 'Pheasant's Eye' looks best growing in drifts with primroses amongst orchard trees, or beneath a hedgerow. The tiny 'Hoop Petticoat' and other midget *Narcissus* are best accommodated as a fringe planting to the pool or wetland.

Though it could be argued that tulips are not suitable for inclusion in a wildlife garden, I could make a very strong case for certain of the species, particularly our one and only native representative. Though *Tulipa sylvestris* is reputed to grow as a woodlander, the best colonies I found in the wild grew as hedgerow plants. Given southern exposure they flower reasonably well and are worth a place anyway as a rare native plant. Other tulips also grow well for me and are eagerly sought after by early flying insects (including bees). *T. tarda* is a very beautiful six inch (15 cm) high species whose creamy white flowers have a deep yellow centre. Also *T. turkestanica*, which carries several white-flushed green blooms to a stem, confounds me by seeding itself down from the rock garden edging the pool into the moister soil amongst the cowslips and snake's head fritillary.

This gives me the excuse and opportunity to expound further about another native bulb which is to me both interesting and beautiful, namely *Fritillaria meleagris*. One of the difficulties encountered by those who aspire to settle the snake's head fritillary in their gardens is that bulbs are often so over-dried before being offered for sale that they are 'dead on arrival' — as a mortician would describe it. Given plump bulbs and a cool soil rich in leaf mould, the chequer board, cup shaped blooms borne aloft on tall (foot-high) stems will offer reward enough to the persistent enquirer.

There is probably less incentive to provide space for summer flowering bulbs. There are so many shrubs, herbs and colourful annuals that, as the young boy said when confronted with a plateful of cream cakes, 'we are spoiled for choice'. Some of the summer flowering bulbs are such excellent food sources for bees, butterflies, and a host of other nectar or pollen seekers, that they are worth growing for that reason alone. *Allium sphaerocephalon* with globular heads of dark red flowers is such a powerful attraction to tortoiseshell and painted lady butterflies that I grow it in several well drained, sunny corners of the garden. *Allium moly*, a low growing species with yellow flowers, makes a good carpeting plant when well sited.

73

The Joy of Wildlife Gardening

Indeed, given the right conditions, 'Spanish moly' (so named because I found this species growing wild on a wooded hillside in Spain), can be a little too assertive in the garden.

The lilies growing in my own garden form so essential a part of the summer tapestry that if they offered only a single sip to a vagrant butterfly they would earn a place. They do more than just this as I discovered when watching hawkmoths busy about the flowers on one particularly slumbrous day when the temperature precluded any inclination to labour other than contemplation. Certainly, the amount of food needed to keep a hawkmoth's wings in motion would need copious draughts of nectar which is an easily converted energy-rich solution of sugars. I grow *Lilium martagon* in all forms, in the hope that one day I shall see hummingbird hawkmoth busy about the flowers as on that memorable day in the Valle de Forescens in France.

For the same nectar and pollen producing reasons, I grow any lily which comes to hand. *Lilium regale* has trumpet-shaped flowers numbering sometimes 20 on each metre-high stem. The petals are white with a purple stain and have a sweet fragrance. *Lilium pyrenaicum* (along with *martagon*), is certainly one of the easiest lilies to please. The yellow turk's cap flowers are generously spotted with black and have a distinctive aroma, described by the more imaginative as an effluva of amorous tom-cat. This particular species was naturalised along a grass path leading to the well in my grandmother's garden, all mixed in with lad's love, so I have a kinder memory of the two mingled into a pleasant pot-pourri.

There is only one absolutely essential requirement for growing lilies, and that is good drainage. Given a porous, free draining and humus-rich soil, lilies are no harder to grow than daffodils. Most lilies grow well in soils which are neutral or slightly acid, though a small number insist on a completely lime-free soil.

Like an artist tentatively experimenting with a palette of colours, autumn adorns a leaf here and there about the garden with scarlet or gold. As if waiting for the introduction, meadow saffron pushes forth goblets of flowers from bare earth or out of tangled roots of grass. Some of the flowers are self-coloured in various shades of pink, rosy lilac or white, while others are chequered. All grow well in most soils, whether acid or alkaline, provided the drainage is good. I plant the corms of all *Colchicum* in August immediately they are available. Sited amongst shrubs with yellow autumn leaf tints they are especially attractive. On average, the planting depth is about 15 cm, and even then, unless top dressed, the corms work their way to the surface. The best in my garden is *Colchicum speciosum* and its varieties which are especially useful for naturalising in grass.

Of the true autumn crocus, I find *Crocus speciosus* the easiest to establish. The enthusiasm with which the dozen bulbs I planted seeded themselves all over the rock garden led to them being banished to the shrub border. The flowers are variously tinted lilac, purple and blue with the segmented orange stigmas adding a curiously jovial contrast. Bumble bees are clumsily busy about the flowers on benign September afternoons, these are possibly mated females building up reserves prior to winter hibernation. Autumn flowers are an especially valuable and nutritious food source for so

BULBS

Anemone blanda varieties 2 in (6 cm). Pink, blue, white, red — spring.

Anemone nemorosa (Wood Anemone) for shade. 2 in (6 m). White.

Chionodoxa luciliae 'Glory of the Snow' 6 in (15 cm). Blue, white — spring.

Crocus Plant especially those flowering in early spring. For naturalising *C tommasinianus* and *augustifolia*.

Eranthus hyemalis and ***Galanthus*** (Aconite and Snowdrop) for early insect forage.

Fritillaria meleagris 'Snake's Head Fritillary' 8 in (20 cm). Pinkish-purple or white, chequerboard flowers — spring.

Muscaria neglectum and ***armeniacum*** 4-6 in (10-15 cm). Purple-blue — spring.

Narcissus (Daffodils) Grow 'Pheasants Eye' (*N poeticus*) and Wild Daffodils (*N pseudonarcissus*). For the rest, their name is legion for there really are so many to choose from.

The splash of colour of Autumn Crocus flowers attracts foraging bees.

Tulipa (Tulips) There are some which in my soil naturalise and are useful insect forage bulbs. Try *T sylvestris* (12 in (30 cm) yellow. *T tarda* 4 in (10 cm) cream on yellow, and *T batalini* 'Bronze Charm' 10 in (20 cm) peach. Plant 6-8 in (15-20 cm) deep.

Summer:

Allium (Ornamental onions) are useful butterfly plants. *A sphaerocephalon* 12 in (30 cm) reddish-purple. *A pulchellum* 12 in (30 cm) violet.

Lilium In suitable conditions *L martagon* and *L pyrenaicum* will naturalise, even in grass. Both are Turk's Cap 36 in (90 cm).

Autumn:

Colchicum autumnale (Meadow Saffron) 6 in (15 cm). Various – September. Best naturalised in grass. *C speciosum* 8 in (20 cm). Rosy-lilac, white. September – October. Best in borders.

Crocus speciosus 6 in (15 cm). Shades of lilac-purple – autumn.

Two others worth a mention, though can be 'miffs and mopes':

Arum italicum 'Pictum' 8 in (20 cm). Marbled leaves, greenish flowers, orange berries.

Leucojum (Summer Snow Flake) 8-22 in (20-44 cm). *L aestivum*, and *L vernum* – white.

many insects which build up reserves of food prior to the onset of winter, such as drone flies on Michaelmas daisies.

Though the *Anemone blanda* bridges the hungry period of March and April in my garden, those who are blessed with a kinder climate insist this is a February flowering species which makes them denizens of winter. This little gem of the buttercup family can be grown from tubers planted under deciduous trees or shrubs during September. In February the finely divided leaves are overgrown by many petalled flowers in shades of blue, violet, pink, white, and more recently carmine. The height is a modest 10 cm, and on warm days the flowers are eagerly sought for by bee flies whose acrobatic, aeronautical skills fascinate me. The bee fly only appears to hover over the flowers of anemone, aconite, crocus, and other vernal blossoms on warm sunny days. In fact, it actually holds on to a petal with its long, spindly legs. I am sure that pied wagtails lurk near the patches of spring flowers because of the abundance of insect life attracted to them.

In the shady areas include small groups of wood anemone, *Anemone nemorosa*. The type plant can be invasive so I grow named varieties, particularly those with blue or pink flowers – namely 'Robinsoniana' and 'Allenii' which are better behaved. Try also the yellow flowered *Anemone ranunculoides*, 'Superba Major' which wanders happily amongst winter cyclamen and dog tooth violet in the shade border, and flowers in early spring.

So much for one half of the instant garden duo, though I have offered only a glimpse of the rich diversity of bulbs. I must be equally parsimonious with annuals which are so expressive of the joyous, profligate days of perennial youth. Like the butterflies they share the careless days of summer while they fill the brief months of existence with an abundance of colour. Certainly no habitat garden will completely fulfil itself without a selection of annuals. I would, however, warn against the over enthusiastic introduction of certain natives – annuals they may be in duration but their offspring ensure a degree of perenniality which makes them immortal – though those that outstay a welcome are usually not difficult to control and, in any event, those weeded out make useful compostable material.

Hardy annuals are useful in that they can be sown direct into their flowering positions outdoors. Half hardy annuals are less obliging and need to be sown under glass, then grown on until all danger of frost is past before being planted out in the garden.

By staggering sowing dates I manage to keep a succession of annuals in flower from mid May to October. The flowers brighten the garden, provide nourishment for insects, and with some species, for example sunflowers and teasels, become a food supply for goldfinches and other seed-eating birds in autumn. Just as an encouragement to the unconverted, a bee-keeping friend of mine maintains that a garden full of *Limnanthes douglasii* keeps his bees fully occupied from May until late August. *Limnanthes*, popularly known as 'foam of the meadow', opens a seemingly endless succession of saucer shaped, yellow edged, white flowers on stems 15 cm high, even when grown in the poorest soils.

The importance of annual flowers as a part of the ecological community cannot be over emphasised. Flowers attract nectar

A selection of colourful garden plants:
Lilium pyrenaicum, Myosotis, Digitalis, Limnanthes, Dianthus, Nicotiana, Centaurea moschata, Phacelia.

sippers and pollen eaters which in turn bring in insect feeding birds, bats, mammals, and a whole range of predators. Swallows and martins hawk low over the flower-filled borders to reap a rich harvest of insects during the long summer days. Then bats plunder the same well filled larder as dusk falls. Without the flowers there would be fewer insects for them to feed on.

The half-hardy annuals can be raised without too much difficulty in a cold greenhouse simply by sowing them a little later. Whereas in a heated greenhouse seed can be sown in February, with only the convenience of a cold house or frame sowing is put back to late April. I cheat a bit by using the kitchen window sills as propagators to germinate seeds of plants which need a longer growing season. After all, why waste all that lovely central heating on mere family.

Having rejoiced in spring by offering borders bright with bulbs, there then comes the problem of hiding the yellowing foliage and bare earth once the last petal fades. Over-sowing the bulb patches with the most resilient of hardy annuals serves my purpose and that of the insects admirably. For dwarf bulbs such as crocus I choose low growing annuals – *Alyssum* 'Carpet of Snow' makes neat mounds of white flowers 15 cm high, which attract more insects, butterflies and other pollinaters than most flowers. Candytuft is another that is useful for sowing amongst *Narcissus* and tulips. Spare a corner also for a patch of wild candytuft, *Iberis amara*, for their mounds of pink and white blooms have a most pleasing scent. It is said to be good as a treatment for that most painful disease, sciatica.

Cornflowers set a cottage garden pattern and make first choice bumble bee feeding places. I also include patches of sweet sultan *Centaurea moschata* 'Imperialis', whose fluffy, sweetly scented flowers in shades of pastel pink, yellow, purple and white attract tortoiseshell butterflies to take refreshment during the day, and dusk flying moths as twilight deepens from the shadows of sunset.

Viper's bugloss (*Echium*), one of those interesting plants whose flowers change colour with age, will flourish in well drained, poor soil. In young flowers the cell sap is acid and the colour pigment red, with age the cell sap becomes neutral or alkaline so the petals turn blue. A similar change occurs with Forget-me-nots (*Myosotis*) which look lovely when allowed to self seed under deciduous shrubs; the mixed shades of dusky blue and pink a foil to the green of young leaf growth. A feature of both forget-me-not and viper's bugloss is the number of great gnat-like flies they harbour – something the dunnock is not slow to take advantage of.

Toad flax (*Linaria*) with their snapdragon-like flowers will, after the first sowing, persist year after year by means of natural regeneration. The height of the flower stems varies from one to two feet (20 cm to half a metre) depending on the variety chosen, though on my wind-swept plot 'Fairy Bouquet', being neatly compact, is first choice.

Foxgloves (*Digitalis*), are quite indispensable plants for shady corners of the garden. Just sowing pinches of seed in odd corners is sufficient to ensure a plentiful supply of the pink spikes of foxgloves. I also grow the 'Excelsior' strain which affords a wider colour range of heavily spotted blooms.

There are flowers with a prima donna complex which makes them

Heather Angel (Biophotos)

if not difficult, a little less easy to grow. Some are, however, so deliciously fragrant that butterflies find them irresistible. *Heliotrope*, the 'Cherry Pie' of childhood, is just such a plant on which I recall butterflies competing with each other for a place on the violet flower heads. 'Marine' is one which grows to over a foot high (46 cm), with deep violet flowers.

In the twilight after a hot day, the garden is a scent-filled retreat.

Painted lady – this beautiful butterfly is an immigrant to Britain from southern Europe.

'Daffodils that come before the swallows dare'

My father apportioned every squeak, rustle, and wind flutter to Pan's People, to allay my childish fears when I accompanied him on his evening walk around the shadow-filled borders. This may explain my affection for plants whose fragrance is particularly evident on still, summer evenings. *Nicotiana* and night-scented stock are just two which I share with the moths.

Many years ago when I kept bees, a man always referred to in the village as Hymi (which I discovered later was short for *Hymenoptera*), advised me to plant *Phacelia campanularia* as what he described as a 'honey breeder'. Indeed, the gentian blue, bell-shaped blooms carried in succession all summer long proved so attractive to me and the bees that I have grown them ever since. Being only 10 inches (25 cm) or so in height, *Phacelia* fits comfortably into a small garden.

Pinks, the *Dianthus* or divine flowers, as Theophrastus writing some 2,200 years ago described them, are garden essentials in my scheme of things. The perennial forms are best known, but being no one to play favourite, I grow the annual varieties like 'Magic Charms', and 'Heddewigii' for the quality of their multi-coloured flowers and in some varieties the boudoir fragrance they distil.

Sweet William deserves a mention as a member of the clan. One of the most vivid memories of the first year my father gave me sole charge of the garden at home was a border 50 feet (18 metres) long planted with dark red sweet Williams. The fragrance from those massed flowers was a better address, as the postman put it, than the name plate on the gate. Sweet Williams are biennial so must be sown and then grown for a year prior to flowering. I like to grow mignonette somewhere near to, though not alongside them, for the two scents have what is best described as a slumbrous, tropical excellence. A pinch of seed dropped onto bare earth, then raked in will suffice. The broad spikes of pinky white, cream or red flowers on foot-high stems are thronged with bees from dawn to dusk, with butterflies contesting a place at table.

Spring usually affords a miser's portion of days warm enough for the windows to be opened wide to give the rooms an airing. A border below the window planted up with wallflowers will permeate the whole house with their gloriously unforgettable fragrance. Where space is limited grow the dwarf varieties like 'Golden', 'Scarlet', 'Primrose', and 'Orange Bedder'. In a grande desmesne, taller varieties – 'Eastern Queen', 'Fire King' which grow to about 18 inches (46 cm) will be suitable. Remember that wallflowers are sown in May to flower the next year.

Some years ago a friend complained that goldfinches no longer visited his garden. I suggested that their absence might be explained by a lack of seeding plants – a result of his wife having taken up flower arranging. Now he leaves a percentage of the Fuller's teasel, sunflowers, and ornamental grass to supply bird food and regenerate themselves by means of self-sown seedlings. The lady of the house looks on those she cuts for arranging as a proper reward for assistance given with weeding and dead-heading.

Think of the garden as a jigsaw, each individual piece filling in a part of the picture. Without bulbs, annuals, and biennials there would be, if not a hole, then a lot of bare earth and a vastly reduced insect larder.

G D Smith

My own pond, dug to resemble a small tarn.

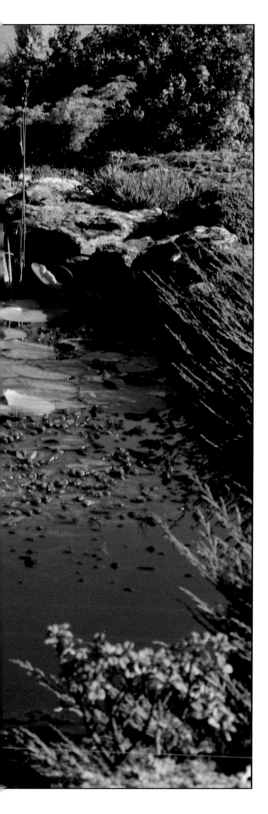

11. Where dragonflies dance

Pools and wet places provide peace and will act as a magnet for all sorts of animals

That we should take time to enjoy every phase of designing, then constructing the garden is essential. For to be in too much of a hurry is to risk making the sort of mistake which could be very costly in both time and labour to put right. Nowhere is the need for careful calculation more vitally important than when considering the how, where, and whyfore of incorporating a stream, pool, or mini-marsh into the design.

To me water is more than just a pleasant feature for it has proved the oasis of life in every landscape that I have had contact with, whether contrived or natural. The village tucked close on the moor edge where I spent my childhood abounded with streams, offering endless possibilities of pleasurable exploitation and exploration to an inquisitive child. Each farm possessed one or several ponds which served as watering places for the domestic animals, and held a teeming abundance of wildlife as well. Out of my own absorbed interest in things aquatic came a growing awareness of how dependent innumerable creatures are on ready access to water: a fact brought even more forcibly home to me when landowners, helped by ever increasing profits began to pipe streams, fill in ponds, and drain wet lands to bring hitherto unworkable acres under the plough. Gone were the moorhens! For all the years of childhood they had built their nest under the now defunct hawthorn by a pond which, sadly, lives only in my memory. The house martins also had to search out a new source of supply of mud for nest building, and the dragonflies became only an iridescent phantom of summers gone by.

It was then, in a gesture of defiance, I built my first pond and still remember the sense of achievement and pride when, only two hours after the pond was filled, a blackbird showed appreciation of my efforts by bathing in the still far-from-clear water. The pond in my present garden is the most persuasive of all inducements just to stand in idle contemplation of the sometimes dramatic, always fascinating, domestic chain of events which are enacted there by the creatures which frequent the area.

The mini-wetland I hoped to create by allowing the overflow from the pond and garage roof to drain into a part of the shrub border did not in practice work, because too late I discovered the subsoil is so free-draining even in winter, that the potential wetland is never more than comfortably moist. A little prior exploration with a spade would have revealed the gritstone underlay. All that was required to make an impervious base to the mini-bog, a sheet of polythene laid 15 inches (37 cms) below the soil surface. Ironically, we learn more from our mistakes than from successful achievements.

Water adds such a bold character to any landscape whether natural or contrived, that unless handled carefully and properly integrated with the other features it can be too dominant. Consider the space available before deciding which water feature will best serve the intended purpose while still merging harmoniously into the overall concept. By doing this initial planning in stages the whole business can be enormously simplified. Mistakes made on paper can be easily rubbed out. Do not be concerned with the suitability or otherwise of the stream, pool, or mini-wet place as a conservation project. In my experience even a semi-permanent puddle is useful, even if it only serves as an ablution or drinking place to the hygiene-conscious avian population.

Let us pause for a moment to think. There are gardens so tiny as to be incapable of accommodating the smallest pond. Think of the possibilities afforded by a bird bath. I know just such a garden which consists of a patio bounded by a narrow shrub border. A most ingeniously contrived bird bath fountain provides anyone watching from the sitting-room window with an enthralling year-round entertainment. The basin is raised on a stone pedestal some 50 inches (125 cm) high. A water pipe leading up the centre of the pillar is so precisely calibrated that half a turn of the tap keeps a three inch (7 cm) high column of water rippling down over the stones laid inside the basin. Surplus water cascades down into a tiny pool and miniscule wet place before draining away to the border. The variety of wildlife which visits the tiny watering place increases with each year that passes. A bird bath, both ornamental and functional, can be contrived from almost anything that will hold water. Once installed, every effort must be made to ensure it is kept filled, for birds and others come to depend on a never failing source of fresh water.

Apart from the limitation imposed by the space available in the garden, our choice of materials will be the major factor to take into account before settling down to planning in detail. Over the years I have constructed pools from puddled clay, concrete, moulded glass fibre, polyester resins and sheet liners. Concrete and puddled clay pools are traditional means of water retention. Both are so difficult to render watertight as to be relegated out of consideration by the introduction of products which are lighter and less laborious to install and which prove more reliable. Moulded glass and polyester resin pools are available in a wide variety of shapes and sizes. They are usually so contoured as to provide ready-made planting ledges, shallow and deep areas. Some even offer the service of ready made edging, though I have never seen this looking anything other than artificial. Care must be taken when installing a pre-formed pool to ensure that sufficient packing material, usually sand, is used to line the hole – or in the case of a raised pool, to back fill so that no gaps are left. Otherwise the weight of water could distort, crack, or weaken the mould so shortening its expected working life of ten to 15 years. Pre-formed pools are quite expensive because of their bulk and complicated manufacturing processes needed to make them. They offer only the most limited opportunity for the expression of individual design

Even the smallest garden, terrace or balcony can offer birds somewhere to drink and bathe. From a small dish or dustbin lid sunk into the ground to elegant troughs and elaborate bowls on plinths, there is something to suit everyone. An attractive and inexpensive birdbath can be made using a plastic planting pot, with a few stones cemented inside to provide different depths of water.

on the gardener's part, except within the limits imposed by the various shapes available. Finally maintaining a healthy balanced water quality is extremely difficult with a small pool.

Having practical experience of all the various methods of holding water I am convinced flexible sheet liners are the best for pool making. They are easier to handle, and need a lot less hard work or skill to install. Even more important from the aesthetic point of view, they permit near complete flexibility in deciding what shape to make the pool or stream.

Deciding on the material to be used completes another phase of the project, and the next point for consideration is which part of the garden will best accommodate what is a very dominant feature. My own technique is to mark out a series of shapes using canes, rope, or if the weather is warm enough to make it flexible, a hose pipe in the various areas of the demesne that are under review. I then keep making adjustments until the right balance is achieved and any last lingering doubt over the rightness of the situation is eliminated. So often after spending hours, on one occasion days, moving pegs, shaping outlines with a hose pipe, even simulating water with a sheet of polythene until frustration almost yielded to helplessness and fury, suddenly the whole disorganised system with a change of just one loop became an harmonious unit, ultimately to become the most satisfying pool I have ever built. Situated on the south-west side of the garden, away from hanging trees, the 9 by 18 ft (3×6 metres) pool has become such a fascinating focus of attention, I had in self defence to partially screen it. It is in view from the house, yet not so close as to interfere in any way with the busy traffic of wildlife.

Always carry a picture in mind of the area as it will look once all the work of construction is completed. The still pool catching cloud reflections, turbulent with passionate frogs in April, coolly persuasive under a July sun, or rippled as a swallow interrupts the patterned geometry of flight to drink. A small cascade, or stream so vibrant with life as to generate immediate sympathy and add a companiable, conversational undertone. Mind images lift the burden of labour and take the ache from tired muscles.

With the dimensions of the pool duly outlined with pegs, hosepipe or cord, you can start digging. Should the site chosen be in an established lawn, skim the turf carefully in strips 12 inches (30 cms) wide by 24 inches (60 cms) long by approximately 1 inch (3 cms) deep. Good quality turf is always useful for patching and repairing damage once the installation works are complete. Removing the turf also reveals the shape in graphic detail and enables final adjustments to be made. Once the first barrow load is removed comes the problem of where to dispose of what will eventually be a large volume of soil. The top spit loam can be spread on existing borders or vegetable plot. The sub-soil is an altogether different matter. Remembering that for fish to be safe from severe frost they need a water depth of 18 inches (45 cms) to shelter in, means there will be a spade depth of sub-soil over the whole area to dispose of. In fact, I dug mine in when preparing shrub and vegetable garden for planting, which is impossible with an established garden. Failing all else, hiring a skip means all the waste soil is removed from the site and disposed of. In my opinion this

The ramshorn snail, a common water snail. Snails will quickly colonise your pond from eggs brought in on the roots of introduced plants. Alternatively, beg a bucket of water from a friend's established pond!

Keith Shackleton

E A Janes

(Left) This rectangular pond dominates a small garden in the heart of London. The elegant little statue is a focal point amidst a jungly profusion of luxuriant plants. Goldfish and pond terrapins inhabit the pond and mallards have been known to make near vertical descents to swim on this tiny oasis!

(Above) In a spell of dry weather a garden pond will come into its own. Here a family of young blue tits gather for a bath – the branch provides a convenient and inviting perch.

is much the best way, rather than trying to turn a heap of glutinous clay into an alpine garden.

Slope the sides at an angle of 20° on clay soil, but on light land the angle may have to be increased until the sides stand without crumbling. There are practical reasons for the sides being cut on the angle like this. The liner will fit snugly on the slope without leaving pockets, and, very important when the pool freezes over, there is room for the ice to expand to relieve the pressure which could cause damage if exerted on a rigid, vertical side. A spirit level and long, straight plank are absolutely vital so that constant checks can be made to ensure the edges are kept level. My first pool, built on a slope, failed in this respect; the top edge was 6 inches (15 cms) higher than the lower, so there was always 6 inches (15 cms) of bare concrete showing to spoil the overall effect. Checks made at intervals across both length and width take up little time and are essential to achieve a pool which fills precisely to the rim all the way round.

Make provision at this stage for marginal plants which need to have their roots in water and leaves in the sun. Some 9 inches (22 cms) below the rim of the pool simply cut a shelf 9 to 15 inches (22-38 cms) wide, then continue with the sloping cut. The shelf can run all the way around the pool, and the marginal plants can be so adjusted as to give a completely natural finish.

The Joy of Wildlife Gardening

Having reached the required depth, say for argument's sake 20 inches (50 cms), crumb out all the loose soil and carefully remove any fragments of glass, pot shards, sharp stones and the like which might punch holes in the liner. Next spread a 2 inch (5 cm) layer of soft builder's sand to form a bed or buffer for the liner to settle down on. My 9 ft by 18 ft (3×6 m) pool needed some 5 cwt (250 kg) of sand to form the cushion, which should be raked and checked for sharp stones during the levelling process.

Now, all was ready for laying the liner which I ordered to size, adding 3 ft (1 m) which is twice the depth of the pool to the length and breadth. This gave me a sheet size of 21 ft by 12 ft (7×4 m). I chose Butyl in preference to PVC simply because it is longer lasting. The prospect of having to remove 5 tons of weather worn limestone and several dozen expensive dwarf conifers, plus the plant and animal content of my pond in order to repair a perished liner was for me sufficient justification for buying the more expensive Butyl.

So to the final stages for which, incidentally, some help will be required if the sheet is bigger than can be comfortably handled. Roll the liner out over the pool so the overlap is roughly equal all round the perimeter, then anchor it in place with paving stones, breeze blocks, or as in my case, pieces of limestone eventually used to build the rock garden.

Now comes the most satisfying stage – dropping the hosepipe into the middle of the liner and turning on the tap to run the water in. Do not be in too big a hurry to bring tea and deck chair for there will be wrinkles in the material to pleat out, anchors to be eased in as the weight of water pulls the liner down into the hole, and most important making certain it settles evenly so the overlap stays equal all round.

To see the pool rim full gives one a tremendous sense of achievement. Then as in my case, the rubber stamp of approval when a sparrow perched on one of the limestone boulders by the pool edge to drink. Already the result of all my labour was rewarded!

How to finish off around the edge is a matter of personal choice influenced by the materials available. I turned the pool into a tarn by cupping it all round in a basin of water worn limestone. By running the outcrops down to the water in several places I made easy access for frogs, newts, birds and other itinerants in need of accommodation. I now realise that the stone would have been better kept to one side, while on the south side the lawn could have been carried right to the rim. Grass to water links the individual units harmoniously together, and provides access to the water for the less nimble mammals.

Before stocking the pond, while the water is maturing so to speak, consider any other embellishments. For example, laying an electric cable so that a small heater can be installed to keep a breathing hole open in the ice which forms during prolonged cold snaps. A breathing hole is essential if fish and plants are to survive the winter and not be asphyxiated by toxic gas given off from rotting vegetation.

Another useful complement to a pool would be a small bog garden for specialist plants and to provide a gradual gradation between the totally aquatic pool and the, by comparison, waterless garden. The wet, swampy area needs to be perennially wet, water saturated

A house sparrow was the first bird to give my pond the seal of approval by coming to drink.

86

rather than merely moist. In fact, with care a bog garden can be contrived which caters for plants which can thrive in a soil so wet that most of the air has been replaced by water, for example yellow monkey musk (*Mimulus luteus*) or those which need dry soil at the crown while the roots are in contact with moist conditions, as do cowslips or water avens. To keep the soil sweet due to a lack of water movement some provision must be made for drainage, or the whole area becomes stagnantly 'aromatic'!

Excavate the soil to whatever depth is necessary to suit the site. In practice I find that erring on the side of generosity works best. As a rough guide a minimum depth of 15 inches (38 cms), with the bottom sloping gently to 24 inches (60 cms) or thereabouts will allow free drainage of water. The base of the excavation can be formed of any impervious material, heavy duty polythene or one of the cheaper pool liners is perfectly adequate for the purpose. Before back filling fit a hose connection through the polythene 9 inches (22 cms) below soil level, leading down through the bog to the lowest point. Another pipe to serve as an outlet can be fitted to drain away stagnant water. Ideally this should be so adjusted as to keep a permanent water table some 6 inches below soil level. Though it may sound complicated in practice the system is quite simple to install. To ensure free water movement a layer of ¾ inch (2 cm) gravel is laid to cover the liner floor. Cover this with coarse peat, reversed turf, leaves, or several thicknesses of newspaper to prevent the soil washing down to block up the gravel drainage. Then top up to ground level with good fibrous loam compost, mixed in the ratio of 5 parts loam to 3 parts peat, 1 part sand. The advantage of a well constructed bog garden is that even in excessively dry weather the moisture level can be maintained just by running water into the bed at the highest point.

There are so many plants which will find conditions in pool and bog garden congenial that unless the choice is made with care, some over robust species may quickly blanket out the whole area. In true conservation terms the choice should be restricted to native plants only. Yet I confess to being not sufficiently strong-minded to do this. Though striving to become an aesthete, and resolved to ignore the beauty of Asiatic primula, Japanese Iris and the architectural quality of Hosta, while concentrating on indigenous or feral plants inevitably my resolve weakens. Non-natives will keep introducing themselves, then charming their way into a place in the garden where, to the purists' chagrin, they co-exist quite happily with the natives. Black fly infest the more exotic water lilies and are eaten with the same alacrity by the insectivorous pond residents when washed into the water with a hosepipe as those from the native yellow and white species. So ignoring the voice of conscience, I balance the two and in so doing provide a manageable, beautiful garden, while making a notable contribution to nature conservancy. For flowers when open, be they native or alien, attract an ever widening range of insects to explore their potential as a food source. Predators follow in a natural succession as anyone who has watched house martins or pipistrelle bats quartering the garden will soon appreciate. Wagtails trip nimble toed from lily pad to lily pad in search of black fly without enquiring the country of origin. Then in August the same birds can be seen like so

The whirring wings and fearless appraising eyes of a large dragonfly make every encounter exciting.

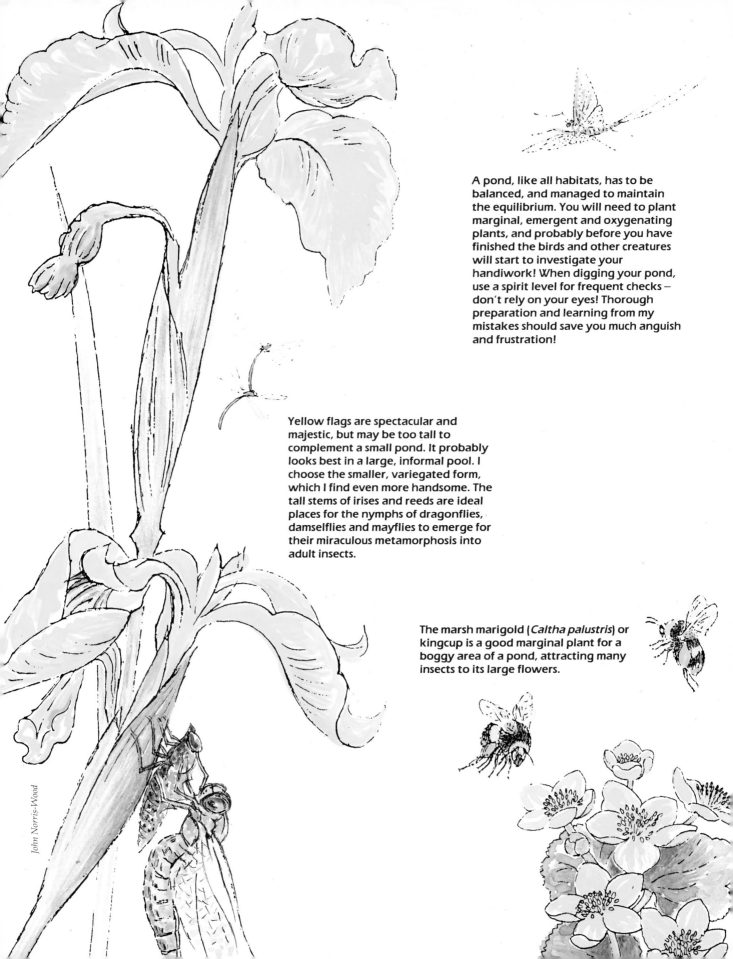

A pond, like all habitats, has to be balanced, and managed to maintain the equilibrium. You will need to plant marginal, emergent and oxygenating plants, and probably before you have finished the birds and other creatures will start to investigate your handiwork! When digging your pond, use a spirit level for frequent checks – don't rely on your eyes! Thorough preparation and learning from my mistakes should save you much anguish and frustration!

Yellow flags are spectacular and majestic, but may be too tall to complement a small pond. It probably looks best in a large, informal pool. I choose the smaller, variegated form, which I find even more handsome. The tall stems of irises and reeds are ideal places for the nymphs of dragonflies, damselflies and mayflies to emerge for their miraculous metamorphosis into adult insects.

The marsh marigold (*Caltha palustris*) or kingcup is a good marginal plant for a boggy area of a pond, attracting many insects to its large flowers.

John Norris-Wood

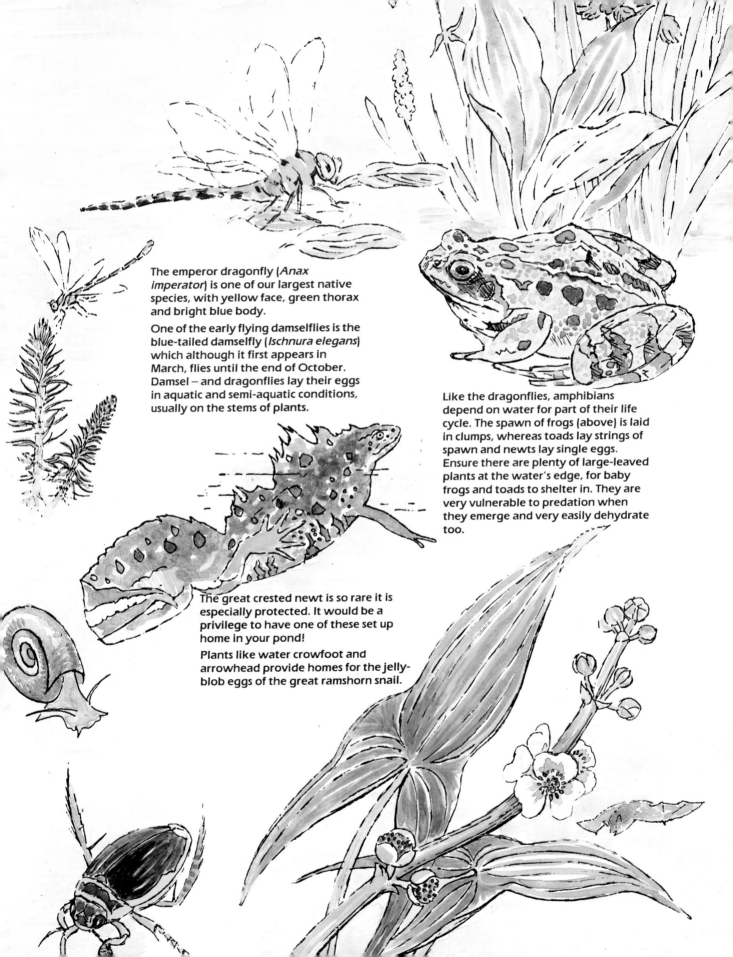

The emperor dragonfly (*Anax imperator*) is one of our largest native species, with yellow face, green thorax and bright blue body.

One of the early flying damselflies is the blue-tailed damselfly (*Ischnura elegans*) which although it first appears in March, flies until the end of October. Damsel – and dragonflies lay their eggs in aquatic and semi-aquatic conditions, usually on the stems of plants.

Like the dragonflies, amphibians depend on water for part of their life cycle. The spawn of frogs (above) is laid in clumps, whereas toads lay strings of spawn and newts lay single eggs. Ensure there are plenty of large-leaved plants at the water's edge, for baby frogs and toads to shelter in. They are very vulnerable to predation when they emerge and very easily dehydrate too.

The great crested newt is so rare it is especially protected. It would be a privilege to have one of these set up home in your pond!

Plants like water crowfoot and arrowhead provide homes for the jelly-blob eggs of the great ramshorn snail.

many clockwork toys bustling around the lawn seizing the egg laying 'Daddy Long Legs'.

Experience has taught me to be extremely circumspect over introducing native plants into the garden. Take for example the aforementioned white (*Nymphaea alba*) and yellow (*Nuphar lutea*) water lilies. I planted both of them along with several garden hybrid *Nymphaea* in a large ornamental pond in my first garden. Within two or three years the water had disappeared under a mask of green leaves, and lovely though the flowers were in due season I had to empty, then replant the pond minus the white and yellow lilies to retain a balance.

Remember, only one-third of the water surface in the pond must be masked by vegetation. Leave the other two-thirds a clear, glinting, reflecting window through which to observe life going on below in the subaquatic depths.

So, instead of the native water lily and spatterdock I would plant imported hardy species or hybrids. Herewith a modest selection: *Nymphaea odorata*, the sweet scented pond lily is well suited for planting in a medium-sized pool at a water depth of 18 inches (45 cms). The fragrant, many petalled flowers measure up to 6 inches (15 cms) across. There is a pink flowered form *N. odorata* 'Rosea' which is of equal quality. The flowers are deep pink with a central boss of yellow stamens and are sweetly scented. This water lily surprised me by producing flowers in mud when the pond they were planted in dried up in the summer of 1975, so the will to survive is obvious. Finally, 'William Shaw', a hybrid which I have planted in my present pond offers fragrant strawberry and cream shaded flowers which it commands approval for by holding them clear of the water.

Of the Laydeker hybrids raised by Marliac of France, specifically for the smaller pools, I would choose *N. laydekeri* 'Purpurata' for the rich textured quality of the red flowers. The water planting depth need be no more than 12 inches (30 cms) and once established this hybrid is the most free-flowering of all. Rather than extend the list further I would suggest consulting one of the specialist catalogues and making a choice from that. I have merely noted my *crème de la crème*.

To maintain a proper healthy balance, plants which are described as oxygenators are of great importance. Some like *Elodea* are rampant weeds, so be careful over planting gifts from neighbours' ponds without seeking first a set of credentials.

Callitriche verna forms dense mats of underwater foliage to perform the dual function of fish protector and oxygenator. The closely related *C. autumnalis* is also to be commended and is particularly useful in winter for keeping the water aerated. *Fortunalis antipyretica*, willow moss, grows a knot of stems covered in moss-like foliage and is invaluable. *Polygonum amphibium* with floating leaves and pink flowers held upright above the water is an essential habitat plant and a native. So is the watercrowfoot (*Ranunculus aquatilis*) with small trefoil leaves and white flowers which I hope might persuade brown china mark moth to breed.

Water violets, like the terrestrial sort, delight me, though they are linked in popular name only. Water violet (*Hottonia palustris*) is an oxygenating plant of merit with fern-like foliage and flowers of white

PLANTS FOR POOLS AND WET PLACES

For shallow pools and bogs:

Caltha palustris – yellow flowers – April.

C palustris 'Plena' – double yellow flowers – April.

Cardamine pratensis – lilac – invasive.

C pratensis flora plena – double lilac – invasive.

Carex stricta Aurea – golden sedge – 2½ ft (75 cm).

Hosta – a wealth to choose from – 6-36 in (15-90 cm).

Lythrum 'The Rocket' – purple – 2-3 ft (60-90 cm).

Myosotis scorpioides, and M palustris 'Mermaid' – blue – summer – 6 in (15 cm).

Mimulus cardinalis – orange-red.

M luteus – yellow – summer – 18 in (45 cm).

M lewisii – pink-red – summer – 18 in (45 cm).

Mimulus hybrids – various forms – 'Scarlet Bee'. 'Ochrid' etc.

Pool margins and water to 12 in (30 cm) deep:

Iris laevigata cultivars – blue, rose etc. June – July – 18 in (45 cm).

I pseudocorus variegata – yellow – July – 3 ft (90 cm).

Menyanthes trifoliata – white – May – 'Bog Bean'. Food for elephant hawk moth.

Pontederia cordata (Pickerel) – blue – July – August – 2 ft (60 cm).

Sagittaria sagittifolia (Arrowhead) – white – July – can be invasive, though not in my pool yet.

Aponogeton distachyus 'Water Hawthorn' – waxy, white flowers, sweetly scented, grows well in deepish water.

Water Lilies:

Nymphaea for shallow water:

N odorata Minor – white – scented.

N Helvola – yellow – lovely foliage.

N Froebelii – crimson – first choice.

Deep water to 3 ft (90 cm):

Nymphaea 'James Brydon' – rose-pink – prime favourite of mine.

N 'Escarboucle' – rich red – select.

N – 'Rose Arey' – soft pink.

Oxygenators:

Callitriche verna – water starwort.

Ceratophyllum demersum – not too invasive or difficult to control.

Elodea crispa – not too invasive or difficult to control.

Hottonia palustris – lilac – June – is a floater and beautiful.

For the broader wetland planting:

Astilbe are excellent flowering with sprays of feathery blooms all summer. Height 3-36 in (8-90 cm) – colour various.

Hosta are available in all shapes, sorts, and sizes.

Iris – particularly forms of *Iris sibirica* – up to 3 ft (90 cm) – blue and white.

Molinia coerulea Variegata is a lovely, non-invasive grass.

Parochetus communis, the 'Clover Pea' galloped and produced a display of electric blue flowers in October, November, then died of frostbite.

Primula – all the wetland sorts. *P rosea* starts the season in March.

P pulverulenta, bulleyana, beesiana, japonica etc continue into summer.

Trollius pumilus and others of the 'Globe Flower' clan.

to violet. Having planted water hyacinth (*Eichhornia*) innumerable times only to have it die, I am forced to the conclusion that in the north at least, the plant is tender. A pity if this is so, for the lavender blue flowers are beautiful, and it makes a most excellent fish nursery. Finally, frog bit (*Hydrocharis*) a floating plant with bright green leaves and pure white, miniature water-lily flowers, irresistible to insects.

Though containerisation now enables planting to be carried out at almost any time of the year, I still choose to do the job in early May whenever this is possible. The specialist nurseries usually dispatch orders to arrive at that time of the year, so it is Hobson's choice anyway. Before planting, do check the list issued by the nursery to find out the best depth of water for the chosen varieties. Aquatics do make a lot of growth in a season so need a nutritious compost to keep them healthy. The bulk is made up with good quality loam mixed with sharp sand, plus a sachet under each root as it is planted of the specially formulated slow release fertilizer. Any container capable of holding compost will serve, though I much prefer to buy the baskets and pans designed specifically for the purpose. Once these are planted up cover the exposed soil with aquarium gravel to prevent it from washing off and clouding the water.

At this point I *should* recommend, as do most books on the subject, that the containers are moved in stages from shallows to deep water. In practice, however, I find putting them straight into permanent quarters makes not the slightest difference to their wellbeing.

Before introducing fish, snails, and putting out the 'pond to let' sign for frogs, newts, and other wanderers in the wilderness, give the water time to mature while choosing plants for fringe and marginal areas. Bog bean (*Menyanthes trifoliata*) lovely denizen of mountain tarns grows well in the shallow pool edge, so immediately the ledge left all round the pool is proved a commendable foresight. The bog bean opens feathery white flowers in July over three lobed blue green leaves. Had my pool been just a little larger, there would certainly have been a place found for the yellow Flag Iris (*Iris pseudacorus*) of the sword like leaves and deep yellow blooms. Unfortunately, the ultimate height of 4 ft (1·22 m) is Brobdingnagian beside my 9 by 18 ft (3×6 m) Lilliputian pool! Instead, choose for limited space the even more handsome variegated form the *Iris pseudoacorus* 'Variegata' which grows only half as tall and flowers in late summer.

Another marginal, cottongrass (*Eriophorum*) conjures up memories of upland plateaux and flower studded tarns. As a consequence, cottongrass is always included in any informal wetland feature I devise. The rush-like foliage bedecks itself in tufted heads of snow-white, silky threads carried on 12 inch (30 cm) stems.

Water forget-me-not though it shows something of an inclination to scramble up onto the limestone ledge behind it is also a handsome wetland plant, only 12 inches (30 cm) high, the flowers pink in the bud opening to blue. There are only a few rush-like foliaged plants to add a contrasting verticle shape to the design. Best of these is flowering rush (*Butomus*) which I first discovered growing wild on the fringe of a farm pond near Worcester. The clusters of pink flowers are carried on stout stems above the tufts of rush-like triangular foliage.

The Joy of Wildlife Gardening

Marsh marigolds grew with the water cress in a beck near my childhood home, so even if it were not one of the most beautiful marginals, sentiment alone warrants not the single flowered form, but rather the double *Caltha palustris* 'Plena'. A 12-inch (30 cm) high mound, of dark green foliage forms a proper contrast to the large double, deep-yellow flowers carried above it.

Though memory is often fallible, and rare treasured moments become polished with the passage of time to a jewelled brilliance, yet an upland meadow I first saw as a teenager, yellow with the flowers of globe flower (*Trollius europaeus*) on a June day proved so compellingly beautiful it has been a place of annual pilgrimage ever since. Globe flowers grow best if planted just out of the water so the roots can reach down to sip as they please. Possibly they are a little tall for the smaller pool at 18 to 20 inches (45-50 cms), in which case *T. pumila* which remains a modest midget of 8 inches (20 cms) or even less is a good choice.

Instead of the native 'common arrow head' I favour the double flowered and very beautiful *Sagittaria japonica* 'Flore Pleno'. Ideally the depth of water above the roots needs to be about 2 or 3 inches (5-8 cms) for the full complement of snow-white, double flowers to be presented for appreciation. Rather tall this one at 24 inches (60 cms) but certainly of the most choice.

Consider for the bog garden a form of loose-strife (*Lythrum salicaria*) known as 'The Rocket', the 3 ft (1 m) spikes of mauve flowers which open in mid summer are a popular food source for bees and certain butterflies.

Common meadow sweet is too large and invasive so I grow the golden leaved form *Filipendula ulmaria* 'Aurea' which though something of a 'miff and mope' is so attractive in leaf and restrained in growth as to be worthy of effort to grow, not least because it attracts so many insects.

Finally, monkey musk (*Mimulus luteus*) which draws a ribbon of yellow on the gravel spits and boggy edges of the stream where years ago I spent hours watching nesting sand martins. From the light green tufts of hairy foliage grow stiff stems, 12 inches (30 cms) high, packed with golden yellow flowers, the moist tangle of roots a haunt of water bugs.

There are so many non-native plants which thrive in a wetland habitat! Asiatic primula and astilbe, by flowering late, offer attraction to a wide range of insects. Hosta or Rheum, have wide umbrella-leaves offer shade and a place secure from predators to young frogs and toads and newts. The leafy refuge provides a slug-rich place to persuade the not over common white-collared water shrew to linger – as happened in my last garden.

Indeed, once the plants have grown in to provide the right conditions it is astonishing how quickly the area becomes populated. Birds, of course, are immediately in evidence drinking, or bathing. I learned from my first pool how often some birds bathe before roosting.

Whirligig beetles, pond skaters, water boatmen, and others came in two water containers from a nearby pond along with frog spawn rescued prior to the land being drained. Blue damselflies, though they took a year to arrive, are now a resident summer feature. Dragonflies,

Water-loving plants: purple loosestrife, *Mimulus luteus*, Hosta, Astilbe simplicifolia, Trollius, Salix, Filipendula ulmaria Aurea, Rheum.

92

like some relic of aviation history, patrol territories, iridescent, fragile and beautiful, at one with the lily flowers wide open to the summer sun.

The water snails I was careful to introduce, both jelly-like eggs and adults. They feed on the algae which form abundantly in all still pools and must be kept within bounds.

Goldfish are not suitable for a pond where frogs, toads, and newts are spawning for they eat the tadpoles. In any future ponds I construct there will be no fish unless they are guaranteed vegetarian.

Never believe the planting is complete. There will be need for change, some plants will be over-invasive, others fail to thrive. A keener appreciation of the needs of a varied inter-dependent community will suggest new plantings. I recently included a bog myrtle, for the dull gold catkins distill a fragrance which assures me of the seasonal change from winter to spring, and dwarf willows, the creeping mat forming *Salix reticulata* and *S. repens*, whose leaves are skeletonised by caterpillars not yet identified, except I am sure by blue tits feeding nestlings.

A pond, stream, or wet place takes time to reach a climatic climax in terms of flora and fauna. There are short cuts which in my opinion are quite permissible so long as facilities provided are suitable, and not just for immediate needs. Frogs, toads, newts, and reptiles can be introduced as eggs yet go through a series of changes not all of them requiring similar environmental conditions. In very cold weather reptiles and amphibians hibernate somewhere safe from frost. Frogs hibernate in mud, toads bury themselves in wet leaves, as do newts which also search out crevices in walls, so the pond for them is essential in two phases – as a breeding place, and for hibernation.

Reptiles, as for example grass snakes, often hunt in ponds, whereas slow worms search for slugs, spiders or worms in the moist seclusion of the leaf-covered bog garden. Grass snakes choose warm places to lay their eggs, which makes a well made compost heap a vital habitat, along with ready access to water. The slow worm giving birth to living young needs a safe maternity ward – in my last garden a heather-covered slope amongst rock outcrops proved adequate.

Pond skaters, whirligig beetles, and water boatmen live out their whole lives near water. Other insects are of a Jekyll and Hyde persuasion. Mosquito larvae, like siphon-breathing threads, are among the first denizens of newly-made ponds, and provide food for several amphibious predators, before taking flight as adults. Dragonfly nymphs, voracious carnivores, use the pond as nursery and dining room during the early part of their lives. Caddis flies also spend their larval phase sub-aquatically.

Without a never-failing supply of water no garden can ever be complete.

12. Bees, butterflies and borders

Hardy, herbaceous perennials are an essential part of any wildlife garden

The very name 'hardy herbaceous perennial' carries a reassuring implication of indestructible durability. For though the top growth dies back each autumn, like some vegetable phoenix rising from the ashes of its own destruction, fresh growth pushes up from the root each spring.

Herbaceous perennials have been part of my gardening life since early childhood. The long border leading the full length of my parents' garden was filled to overflowing with old-fashioned herbaceous perennials. Monkshood, geraniums, golden rod, chimney bell flower, stonecrop and the like, added colour in their season. Waiting until a bumble bee crawled into a monkshood flower then pressing the cape shut offered a variation on the jam jar trap as an after school pursuit. A flower-packed border which in those unpolluted days was so busily populated with insect life that their conversational foraging added a lazy undertone to many a warm summers day. Where my professional training began, there was a double herbaceous border running the full length of a walled garden. There, from when the first flowers on *Aubretia* and *Alyssum* opened in April until the Michaelmas daisy withered in October, insects of one sort or another fed busily on the bounty offered. This particular garden played host to possibly the most varied collection of bugs, butterflies and insects I have ever seen. On the walls surrounding the garden there were fruit trees: apples, plums, morello cherries, roses, and other wall plants. This, combined with the herbaceous border and shelter from the wind, made the place a bird and insect haven.

Time has blurred my memory so that the salient features of many of the varied borders I have designed then planted with herbaceous perennials have coalesced. Arguments over, or comparisons with, the merits of traditional one-sided borders with a minimum width of 14 ft (3·5 m), and the advantages offered by island beds are resolved due to the limitation imposed by the space available and personal preference with regard to plants. After years of tending beds and borders planted only with true herbaceous perennials, I gradually progressed to a mixed culture system. The herbaceous border as such contributes little to the landscape, or as a larder to birds, insects and other animals during the winter. I now prefer to group the herbaceous with shrubs and annuals in a cottage garden style mixed border. This is more effective in landscape terms and infinitely better as wildlife habitat, being closer to the coppice and hedgerow terrain of the open countryside. For in addition to providing a suitably varied food supply, the garden needs to offer readily accessible cover as protection from

The herbaceous border in the formal gardens at the RSPB's headquarters at The Lodge provides colour throughout the year and attracts butterflies and other insects. Wistaria climbs the walls of the building.

The Joy of Wildlife Gardening

predators. This is why the feeding places, bird table, nut dispensers and other winter aids provided here are sited conveniently close to shelter, yet not so close as to be within pouncing range of a cat. In the back garden an enormous holly tree offers a safe retreat when a sparrowhawk whips down the hedge line and over the wall. In the front garden a dunnock, thrush, or blackbird can dive for cover into a tangle of shrubs. Herbaceous plants chosen for the quality of flower or beauty of foliage add much to the attractiveness of our gardens and surrounding countryside, so I select with the same care as that exercised by a Solomon making up the numbers in his harem.

There are herbaceous perennials available to suit almost every soil type and situation. Some are so desperately eager to please they quickly over-run the garden unless disciplined. Others are so fastidiously exacting in regard to soil and situation as to require cajoling to accept our hospitality. The best time for planting depends on the location of the garden and type of soil. In a northern garden blessed with a heavy moisture—retentive clay soil I would prefer spring planting. Otherwise, anytime between October and early April when soil condition and prevailing weather enable the work to be carried out in comfort will suit nicely.

Many years ago I laid down a herbaceous border in the garden surrounding a house which was two hundred years old. The soil, after being worked for decades would, as the cognoscenti of gardening describe it, have grown walking sticks. Unfortunately, the site included two very tenacious perennial weeds – ground elder, and *Convolvulus*. In spite of grave misgivings, I was persuaded to plant up the border before time proved all the weed had been removed. Within two years weeds and plants were so inextricably mixed the whole lot had to be dug out, burned, and the border put down to grass.

Before planting make sure every scrap of weed has gone. The pure-blooded garden observer will argue weeds are part of the overall habitat – all I would say is – in *their* garden, not mine! I still have dreams of *Convolvulus* reaching out tentacles over delphiniums, and bishop weed co-habiting too closely with *Dianthus*: rather like introducing a scrub bull into a pedigree dairy herd – the results of the mis-alliance take time to show themselves.

There is one other consideration which influences those who would share park and pasturage with a wide selection of wildlife, and that is the value of the plants chosen to provide food and cover. Fortunately, the number of herbaceous perennials which are useful and beautiful offers enough of a selection to replant Eden.

The plants growing in the wall fronting the terrace are more alpine than herbaceous yet are such an excellent feature I include them here. *Aubrieta, Alyssum, Saxifraga*, thrift, and several other spring-blooming, low-growing plants turn a hollow wall and table bed into a spring festival as they erupt into flower. The cracks between the stones give root hold for *Erinus alpinus, Linaria*, and *Arabis*. There, sheltered from the wind, plants flower a fortnight earlier than in the open ground. Tortoiseshell butterflies, honeybees, and other flower dependent insects tempted by a few days of mild weather make good use of the facilities offered by the wall. A pair of wrens which nest

Herbaceous perennials, including crane's bill, *Alchemilla mollis*, bugle, *Sedum*, *Aubrieta*, *Alyssum*, *Aconitum*, *Campanula latifolia, C lactiflora*, yellow loosestrife.

each year in the ivy-covered well at one end of the table bed, spend most of the short winter days feeding along the wall and shrub border below it. That I am persuaded also to linger long to enjoy winter sunshine while watching the busy trafficking amongst the flowers makes it no less of a feature. I have planted the border below with bugle (*Ajuga*), lungwort (*Pulmonaria*) and a selection of *Sedum* and *Sempervivum* to continue the floral tribute and mark the passing seasons, so the supply of pollen and nectar is continuous almost from February to October.

Though my preference is to use herbaceous perennials as an integrated part of the overall design, a border either single sided or island bed is the garden tradition. By making a careful selection from the list of plants available a border can be contrived to offer colour for at least ten months of the year.

Let the season begin as it does in my garden with 'Christmas roses' to welcome in the new year. I grow *Helleborus niger* in a leaf mould soil in a north facing border where it can spread self-sown seedlings around and about. At least those seeds which are overlooked by bank voles get the opportunity to germinate. Possibly the bank voles are encouraged by the mixed corn scattered around the bird-table. Certainly the little owl that roosts in the overgrown copse finds this area a profitable hunting ground; three pieces of the habitat jig-saw which perfectly interlock. The various forms of *Helleborus orientalis*, and *H. abschasicus* carry the torch until *H. corsicus* lifts the garden into March and springtime.

Spring is a chemistry of so many things – flower colour, leaf tones, light and shade, plus the feverishly procreative life of the mobile inhabitants of the garden – a series of individual compositions linked together by interdependence into a unified whole.

There are many mini-woodland scenes using a tree or tall shrub as a central feature with a herbaceous ground cover. A silver birch grown from seed to 18 ft (5·5 m) high in 12 years is part of a native copse complex. Lady's mantle (*Alchemilla*) growing close about the birch bole with distinctive pale green leaves and yellowish green flowers makes exceptionally effective ground cover. The leaves carry droplets of dew to catch and reflect sunlight – a horn spoonful of this leaf moisture, so legend has it, will turn base metal to gold.

Primroses play a part in the spring composition, and marsh marigold (*Caltha*) grows alongside water avens (*Geum*) in moist soils near the lawn edge together with leopard's bane (*Doronicum*). Because this mini-woodland affords a safe retreat to the young frogs as they leave the pool I have planted several *Hosta*, the thick leaf canopy makes a secure hiding place and beautifies the garden. A scattering of foxgloves completes the ensemble except for the violets which I hope one day will tempt dark green fritillary from the coast.

There are plants which make such prime hosts to specific insects that they must be added to the prospectus. I persuade myself that in this exceedingly chilly garden, given a healthy stock of rock rose (*Helianthemum*) and various *Geranium* (Crane's bill), the rare and lovely brown argus butterfly might find climate and hospitality acceptable. I grow yarrow, though not the common *Achillea millefolium* except as an uninvited guest in the lawn. Instead I prefer

HERBACEOUS PERENNIALS

Achillea Galaxy hybrids 3 ft (60-90 cm). Pink to yellow – summer.

Achillea 'Moonshine' 2 ft (60 cm). Yellow – early summer.

Aster – amellus hybrids 1-2 ft (30-60 cm). Colours vary – late summer.

Aster x frikarti 3 ft (90 cm). Lavender-blue – summer to autumn.

Aster novae-angliae 3 ft (1 m). Mauve – late summer.

Aster novi-belgi (Michaelmas Daisy) 18-36 in (46 cm-1.2 m). Colours vary – late summer.

Astilbe In moist soils as a foraging ground for seed and insect eaters.

Campanula (Bell Flowers) 2-36 in (4 cm-1 m) Large family, grow all according to personal taste. Colours various – summer.

Centaurea (Cornflower) 2 ft (60 cm). Pink, blue, white – summer.

Geranium Excellent, easily grown perennials – include all that fancy dictates.

Hosta To provide moist shade for foragers – bird, animal, reptile.

Lamium maculatum vars. Foliage ground cover. White, blue, or pink flowers.

Lysimachia punctata (Yellow Loosestrife) 3 ft (90 cm). Yellow flowers – April – May.

Lythrum 'The Beacon' 3 ft (90 cm). Rosy-red summer.

Nepeta (Catmint) Six Hills 2 ft (60 cm). Summer.

Polygonatum 'Solomons Seal' 30 in (75 cm).

P Multiflorum White. May – June.

Polygonum affine 'Darjeeling Red' 8-10 in (25 cm). Carpeting plant, red – late summer.

Pulmonaria 'Lungwort' 18 in (25-35 cm). Forms of *angustifolia* and *saccharata*. Pink – blue – spring.

Sedum rhodiola (Rose Root) 10 in (25 cm). Yellow – spring.

Sedum spectabile vars. 12-24 in (30-60 cm). Large heads, pink flowers. September – October.

Veronica spicata and *tectorium* vars. 8-16 in (20-40 cm). Blue, purple, pink – summer.

Bumblebees live in small colonies. The queen bees come out of hibernation on a warm day in spring and, after feeding, will seek out an old mouse nest in which to lay her eggs.

the modern hybrids 'Moonshine', and 'Galaxy' hybrids with flowers in shades of yellow, pink, and red. All are easy to cultivate and grow to about 36 inches (just under a metre) high. They look handsome in association with monkshood, *Aconitum napellus*, and *A. ivorine* which are both easily raised from seed and are much favoured by red-tailed bumble bees (*Bombus lapidarius*) if memories of childhood serve me correctly. In any event, monkshood are easily grown trouble-free perennials ranging in height from 18 inches to 60 inches (46 cm to 1·5 metres).

Plants with daisy flowers are to my mind particularly suitable, for every aspect of the interaction between insect and host is plainly visible. Watching an enormous bumble bee wallowing on a *Centaurea dealbata* 'Stenbergii' flower and getting covered in pollen at the same time adds another meaning to the phrase 'gluttonous enjoyment'. The perennial cornflower, *Centaurea*, grows wild in the unmown lane verges near my home.

Michaelmas daisy is another of similar flower style and I grow several of the *Aster novi-belgii* just for the butterflies to feed on during those warm, sunlit days which September's Indian summer affords. Where mildew proves a problem, as it frequently does in sheltered gardens, then the *Aster amellus* varieties 'King George', 'Nocturn', 'Violet Queen', and the *novae-angliae* 'Autumn Snow', and 'September Ruby' will serve the garden equally well and are less prone to the ubiquitous mildew. Not all asters flower in late summer, several are excellent for mid-summer colour. *Aster thomsonii* 'Nana' carries a crop of lavender blue flowers through June and July, and makes a useful 16 inch (40 cm) high front of the border plant. I like *Aster frikartii* 'Monch' for the lavender blue flowers which open on 28 inch (71 cm) high stems all through the summer into autumn. My affection for this species is a relic of childhood for I saw a white-letter hairstreak butterfly resting on one. Thereafter, I spent hours searching the elms which sheltered one side of my garden in Norfolk for more eggs or adults. That particular hairstreak, never common even in that near ideal habitat, vanished with the elms even before aerial spraying became common practice.

Though I would hesitate to suggest planting ragwort in a well tilled soil, both the type species *Senecio jacobaea* and the introduced Oxford ragwort (*S. squalidus*) are attractive enough to earn a place in the wild flower corner. Some fields near my house show great patches of yellow ragwort flowers from spring to autumn. In Norfolk, I have seen dozens of black and yellow cinnabar moth caterpillars feeding on ragwort yet have found only one colony here in 1963.

The well designed and constructed herbaceous border should have undulations of tall plants brought forward to the front. Plants which flower late in the season would need to be so placed as to grow up and hide the yellowing foliage of those courageous enough to open their buds in early spring.

Campanula, the lovely mid-season flowering bell flower, is indispensable both for garden decoration and attracting insects to the garden. I grow all that come my way, from harebells on a steep slope in the wilderness corner, through alpine species like *C. carpatica* which grow 10 inches (25 cm) high, to the herbaceous giants. Try

Foxgloves with poppies and ox-eye daisies.

C. glomerata 'Superba' with forms of *C. lactiflora* and the lovely *C. latifolia* 'White Ladies' growing with meadow crane's bill. *Geranium pratense* 'Kendal Clarke' along with yellow loosestrife, *Lysimachea punctata*, and *Lythrum* 'The Beacon'. I know the mixture sounds luxuriously extravagant yet it is the best foraging ground for wildlife in the garden, and the least expensive.

There is a lane, one of my favourite haunts nearby, where several of the plants listed grow wild; harebells in a bed of bilberry, meadow crane's-bill, yellow loosestrife, and willowherb with blackberry, that most excellent food plant, forming thickets over the grey stone walls. As if this were not enough, at intervals on both sides of the lane there are hawthorns and rowans. At all seasons it is lovely. In autumn, a view to the west of purple-shaded moor and to the east of field-patterned dale achieves a beauty which beggars description. Add acres of unsprayed fields and moors plus a varied selection of wildlife and it becomes a treasured fragment of the countryside of my childhood. Last April I counted 304 curlews feeding on the wet meadow below the lane, and only yesterday I watched goldfinches at work on the seed thistle heads. Given care with planting, a garden can offer similar harbourage.

As a result of my infatuation with this particular lane I introduced all the plants to be found growing there into the garden with the exception of the full-sized rowan. Instead, I planted the dwarf form *Sorbus aucuparia* 'Fastigiata'.

There are so many herbaceous plants which are clamouring (if flowers and utility have a voice). None are more eminently suitable than the *Sedums*, for they attract the attention of a greater variety of insects – particularly bees, butterflies, and moths – even than *Buddleia*. To begin with I grow *Sedum spurium*, *S. floriferum*, and *S. spathulifolium* in a gravel path. They flower with a glad abandonment which commands applause and every bee, hoverfly, and butterfly join company to take nourishment from them. In Autumn, who, having once witnessed it, will deny the qualities of *Sedum spectabile* 'Autumn Joy'. In summer the waxed succulence of the leaf is followed by the wide heads of salmon pink flowers, clustered so thickly with feeding insects on occasions as to form an ever-changing pattern.

Of 'golden rod' (*Solidago*) I would suggest planting only the modern varieties – 'Cloth of Gold', 'Crown of Rays', and the diminutive 'Golden Thumb'. Who knows, with knapweed, yarrow, and ragwort already growing in the garden, the variety of moths could include the lime speck pug which so closely resembles the visiting card of a loose-bowelled pigeon.

Let me conclude as I started by emphasising that herbaceous plants are an essential component part of a conservation garden.

13. Garden pot-pourri

Plant for fragrance to enhance the evening air and ensure a wide variety of garden visitors

A garden filled with the colour of flowers should be a blend of perfumes also, otherwise the effort is no more than a compilation of colours, a mere artistic impression. There is nothing more evocative or memory stimulating – or in the case of some plants, exhilarating – than scent. The handful of lavender flowers plucked and tucked down my shirt front when mowing seemingly endless vistas of lawns as a teenager, have ensured the fragrance of this most cottage garden of flowers a place in my affections for ever. The cool, fresh, lemon scent of *Dictamnus albus*, merely a leaf or petal crushed between my fingers lifting the bone-weary, yet happy tiredness of a day turf cutting on the moor edge. That same sharp citrus scent still refreshes me, mind and body. A plant of lad's love (*Artemesia*) grew near the front gate of my childhood home and it was my habit to snatch a sprig on my way from school. Combine this with the scent of burning peat and birch logs and there is conjured up from memory a sense of the warm, secure, innocent enjoyment of childhood in a dales village.

Scent then, is to me as essential a part of garden design as flower colour, leaf shape, or plant form. Indeed, I raised the well wall exactly nineteen inches (48 cm) above general garden level because that, for me, is a comfortable sitting height. Before taking my ease, when the day has been hot, I just damp the plants over, and the distillation from leaf and flower like some beautifully blended pot pourri steals me time from Eden. To each of us scent will have a different ability to attract or repel; stimulating, thought-provoking or nostalgia inducing, yet always adding that prime element necessary for the full enjoyment of any garden, large or small.

One of the most remarkable plants growing within nose scent of my well wall is an *Ozothamnus ledifolius* (Tasmanian lacquer bush) which fills the air all round with the mouth watering aroma of freshly made strawberry jam. By accident, I discovered the resinously fruity smell of the *Arbor-vitae* mingles most agreeably with that of the lacquer bush. I am sorely tempted to copy a planting scheme I saw recently, even to the extent of rooting cuttings to form the basis of a patio hedge. The design had as a backing, a hedge of *Arbor-vitae (Thuja plicata)*, possibly best known as western red cedar. The variety used was called 'Fastigiata' which needs little more than light trimming to keep it in good order. Clipped during early August it made a fragrant screen to a small terrace. Various containers were arranged about the flagged area, and a hollow wall separated terrace from wall and lawn. The containers were filled with plants noted for their fragrance, and were changed as the seasons passed one into another.

The Joy of Wildlife Gardening

Spring was for the boudoir-scented *Hyacinths* and the musky aroma of wallflowers. I remember also an enormous specimen of a *Rhododendron fragrantissimum* whose delicate shaded, apple-pink flowers are so exceedingly fragrant. For twenty years and more this specimen spent winters in a cold greenhouse and summer outside on the terrace. In summer, as fancy dictated, there were pots of garden pinks with 'Mrs Sinkins' a prime favourite. I remember also a time when *Nicotiana* 'Evening Fragrance' transformed the half dark of a warm summer midnight into a Mediterranean experience.

There are plants which I find remarkable, simply because they have added so much pleasure to my gardening life. One such plant is *Heliotrope peruviana*, known as Cherry Pie to so many of those who, like myself, trained in the now near-extinct private gardens. In those halcyon days I grew sweet peas both for my own and my father's pleasure. Although their flowers possessed no show potential, they distilled the most extravagant scent. Varieties like 'Matucana', 'Painted Lady', and 'Queen of the Blues' are particularly good.

Evening is the time when scent is most intrusively persuasive of its presence. As the westering sun throws cool shades across the garden, a mood of reflective quiet allows a proper appreciation of scent. *Datura*, those elegant relatives of the potato, make fine patio plants. The large trumpet-shaped flowers have a sweet almost cloying scent most evident as the twilight deepens. *Datura*, like the *Heliotrope*, need to be moved indoors for winter.

I always grow just a few of that most fragrant, trumpet-flowered 'Regal Lily' in pots for use as patio decoration. This is an easy lily to grow from seed: the ivory-white flowers stained purple outside and flushed yellow in the throat are imbued with a most distinctive perfume. Grow nearby one of the musk roses called 'Felicia', and the excellent 'Zépherine Drouhin' in tubs for training up onto a trellis where the quality and odour of the flowers can mingle and be best appreciated. I have a framework made for the tub to sit on, which supports the trellis almost with the same rigidity as a wall. There are so many very fragrant roses, both ancient and modern, that only personal preference enables a selection to be made. My only advice here would be to choose the rose with your eyes shut, for a rose without a scent is a mere mirage.

Calamintha nepetoides is a long-flowered, much underrated plant. The tiny, lilac flowers appear from mid-summer into autumn, and bees find them irresistible. I plant it close to steps, for the leaves when crushed, or even brushed against, give off a minty perfume. As the height is only 12-18 inches (30-46 cm), *Calamintha* also makes a good plant for crevices in paving.

Even in mid-winter, there are often days when being outdoors is a pleasure, not an endurance test. Just for these occasional days when winter steals summer's glory, I grow *Daphne mezereum* 'Rosea' in a pot close against the house wall. What *is* surprising, is just how many insects are, like me, tempted out to enjoy the pallid sunshine. Unfortunately, unlike the bees, I cannot sample the flowers' bounty. Then in July, greenfinches which eagerly eat the green berries on *Daphne* growing elsewhere in the garden, leave those on the container plant to ripen fully for the blackbirds to enjoy. In the small bed, *Daphne*

Small tortoiseshell on lavender.

104

Heather Angel

retusa forms a 15 inch (38 cm) high evergreen molehill embroidered in May and June with deep, rose-purple flowers.

Grow those plants with special qualities, for example early flowering or outstanding perfume, in a sheltered corner, so each degree of excellence can be enjoyed in comfort by all who enquire. So when considering what to plant as part of the scenery, consult everyone from youngest to eldest on which things to choose. Honeysuckle grows so abundantly in hedgerows that I never thought of planting any in the garden. Not, that is, until my wife pointed out that not everyone is prepared to walk around the lanes as I do, inhaling like a disorientated pointer dog. I promptly took cuttings from the best form of *Lonicera periclymenum* I could find. Once rooted they were planted so as to tumble over the wall by the front gate. The flowers of honeysuckle are cream, then yellow after being fertilized, and the unforgettable fragrance is my favourite after that of the primrose. The moths which gather to feed on the flowers at dusk offer a useful diversion from leaning one's elbows on the gate. I have a suspicion that the little owl from the copse was interested in more than the honeysuckle perfume on several occasions, though even a plump moth would offer no more than a taster. The scarlet berries are eagerly sought after by blackbirds in particular. That it is also a popular nesting site makes honeysuckle a very useful climber.

I first discovered belladonna lilies (*Amaryllis belladonna*) during my species only gardening phase. The long, elegantly formed, pink trumpet flowers, filled to overflowing a narrow border edging a flagged walk. With no leaves visible they made a picture in late August sunshine that was quite unique in my experience. It was the fragrance which intrigued me and to this day I can not decide whether it reminds me of ripe apricots or nutmeg flower. The sun-warmed wall above was dotted with butterflies sunbathing, presumably after feeding, although I was assured by my guide that moths were the most addicted pollinators. A warm wall is absolutely essential, so I grow my *Amaryllis belladonna* in tubs then move them into a cold greenhouse for the winter.

Often our liking for a plant derives from the mood and context of where we first saw it. Certainly, this is often the case so far as I am concerned. Take for example, *Geranium macrorrhizum*, associated always in my memory with Mount Olympus and that notable, yet difficult rock plant, *Jankaea*, which I was searching for at the time. I found the *Geranium* instead growing beside a waterfall cascade: the fragrance from the moist leaves was evident long before I scrambled up the ledge to where it was growing. The smell of *Geranium* leaves is one you either like or dislike, so sniff before buying. I grow a form known as 'Ingwersens variety', with deep pink flowers and leaves which turn vivid scarlet in autumn.

Certainly context and the association of one plant with another combined to fix *Wistaria* and winter iris (*Iris unguicularis*) indelibly in my memory. The setting was an old stableyard which had been cleverly converted to a most tasteful sitting out and picnic place. Long before the barbecue became popular, meals were cooked there on warm evenings and eaten outdoors. A *Wistaria* covered the whole of the wall 50 ft (15 m) long, and in May-June when the wall disappeared behind a curtain of lilac blue flowers the courtyard filled up with their perfume. I remember also there was an 'Albertine' rose covering another wall whose first coppery apricot flowers opened as those of the *Wistaria* ended, and another scent was added to that of toasting sausages. The south-facing border under the wall was filled with three different varieties of winter iris growing in a raised bed, so the scent could be enjoyed by all who walked or sat near them. I have only once seen winter iris flowering so profusely as those in that sheltered ex-stableyard and that was in a garden on Jersey. There, conditions were similar, a soil laced with crushed oystershell in perfect drainage, the bed facing south at the base of a wall.

Romneya coulteri cannot be guaranteed completely hardy for in my present garden top growth gets cut back to soil level by hard frost. Fresh shoots grow at an astonishing rate as the weather warms.

ANNUALS – BIENNIALS

Alyssum 4 in (10 cm). For colour, scent and free-flowering – summer.

Antirrhinum Just for the bumble bees to plunder, various colours and heights.

Arabis alpina 6 in (15 cm). Grown as biennial trailer, pink and white – summer.

Calendula (Marigold) 12-24 in (30-60 cm). Fun plants – just sow and step back. Can be used as a herb, will bloom every month out of the twelve. Shades of yellow and orange.

Centaurea moschata Sweet Sultan 24 in (60 cm). Colours various – scented.

Centaurea cyanus Cornflower 24 in (60 cm). Blue, or in hybrids red-rose, blue and white.

Cheiranthus Wallflower 18 in (45 cm). Biennial, colours various – glorious scent.

Digitalis (Foxglove) hybrids 5 ft (15 cm).

Echium (Vipers Buglos) 12 in (30 cm). Mid-blue.

Geranium robertianum (Herb Robert) 4 in (10 cm). Deep red, spreading.

Helianthus annuus Sunflower 4-9 ft (120-270 cm) Yellow flowers, abundant seed for finches to plunder.

Iberis Candytuft 6 in (15 cm). Easy to grow, just sow where they are to grow – various.

Larkspur (Delphinium consolida) 3 ft (90 cm). Blue, in hybrids various.

Limnanthus douglasii (Foam of the Meadow) 6 in (15 cm). An exceptional bee plant. Yellow and white.

Lunaria (Honesty) 3 in (60 cm). Purple.

Matthiola bicornis Night-scented stock 12 in (30 cm). Lilac – just for fragrance at dusk.

Nicotiana (Tobacco plant) 'Evening Fragrance' 30 in (75 cm). Various.

Nigella Love-in-a-mist 18 in (45 cm). Blue, good seed-heads.

Phacelia campanularia 6-8 in (15–23 cm). Blue. Bee plant.

Reseda Mignonette 15 in (38 cm). Greenish-yellow – again, for the fragrance.

Romneya – the tree poppy – has shared gardens with me since childhood. The large, solitary white flowers with a tangled mass of yellow stamens at the centre just invited a child to bury his face in them to inhale their subtle fragrance. Not until middle age did I appreciate what a splendid courtyard plant *Romneya* can be when given the opportunity. The day had been long, searching for *Delphinium cardinale* across miles of alkali-dusted and poison oak encrusted Californian hillside. On the five mile walk back to the motel I called at the Mission of San Antonio for refreshment. Imagine stepping from hot greyness into a cool, moist garden filled with the refreshing tinkle of fountains, great masses of flowers and across the front of the building an enormous bed of tree poppy in full bloom. The scent from hundreds of full open flowers mingled with that of roses and herbs was beyond telling. I was so lost in admiration that a voice asking me if the owner could be of help nearly made me jump out of my alkali encrusted boots. I grow the *Romneya* and love it, though the insects which cluster on the flowers lack the vivid character of those I saw in San Antonio.

As the sun sets and the light leaves the garden so flower colours change. The darker shades of red and blue fade into the general leaf pattern, while the pale yellow and white blooms gather light to themselves becoming focal points in the garden. The value of grey foliage becomes apparent as I discovered when turning a corner and coming unexpectedly on a group of *Eryngium* 'Miss Willmott's ghost' and Madonna Lily *Lilium candidum*. For a brief moment all the ghost stories were condensed into stark reality and the Barguest (the ghost of the Yorkshire dales) no figment of folklore. Then I caught the fragrance of lily, so subtle that it persuades rather than assaults the senses. One of the memorable experiences of travelling worldwide in search of flowers focussed on the Madonna Lily. As with the Tree Poppy I had walked several miles across a hillside like a limestone pavement only infinitely more dangerous. The sun was so hot even the tortoise had moved into the shade. Then as I climbed over the hill and looked down on the other side, there were the lilies, singly and in clusters, growing out of earth-filled cracks in the stone. Thousands of the pure white flowers filled the air with their unmistakable perfume. I sat down to watch as twilight masked all other detail and only the flowers were left glowing, luminous, across the hillside. As the air cooled so the scent became stronger and suddenly the sky was filled with flickering shapes of moths, and bats which my companion identified as Mediterranean horseshoe bats.

Lilac has only flower quality and fragrance to recommend it as a garden plant so I take care to position it accordingly. My plants of white lilac were raised from cuttings taken from a bush which my grandmother planted as a very young bride in her first garden. Grown as a standard and planted around with *Delphiniums* I can enjoy the colour and scent of the flowers before the *Delphiniums* grow up to mask the shrub's mediocrity when not in flower.

The perfume of flowers is far sweeter on the cooling air of evening than during the hot afternoon. Group those with the most appealing fragrance close around the house, or use to edge a much-used path, for their joy – like summer – is short-lived.

14. Cover story

Ground cover plants have the attraction of reducing the gardener's work, while providing protection and feeding grounds for small creatures and birds

Heathers are ideal ground cover.

I am still searching for plants, other than those classified as weeds, which are ornamental and yet at the same time form a thick enough canopy to exclude competition and so deserve the title ground cover.

There are several plants which I have discovered in my search for the utopia of a weed-free garden which nearly meet the requirements. Various forms of juniper – particularly the Pfitzers (*Juniperus x media* 'Pfitzeriana') come close to the twin ideals of beauty and weed suppression. Yet those 'black knights' in the jousting list – bindweed, couch, ground elder, and in my garden a pernicious violet, are still capable of maintaining a presence even under a juniper.

The best form of ground cover is a border filled with bedding plants which will suppress weeds for a season, and can then be removed, leaving the soil to be thoroughly cleaned and renovated.

Heathers almost fill the twin criteria of ornaments and weed suppressors. They are also very good for wildlife. Unfortunately, apart from a select few, they are extremely fastidious in their soil requirements, which must be lime-free. Some species of *Erica* will attempt to grow, if not thrive, in an alkaline soil providing it is well mulched with peat. Plants of the variety, including the lovely 'Myretoun Ruby' with glowing red flowers, are lime-tolerant. So too are the *Erica x darleyensis*, and *Erica erigena* which, like *carnea*, both flower in winter through to late April. Only one summer-flowering heath, *Erica stricta* has proved adaptable enough to cope with a lime soil, but it is upright in growth and so not much use as ground cover. Given an acid soil with all the vast legions of *Calluna* and *Erica* at our command then a heather garden will provide year-round flowers, a 'Joseph's coat' of many-coloured foliage, and the sort of cover that insects, spiders, some birds, reptiles, and sundry mammals thoroughly approve of.

Heathers alone do not show sufficient variation in height and texture to make a landscape interesting, I use so-called 'dwarf' conifers, certain shrubs which flower and berry, plus a whole range of bulbs and herbaceous plants to make up the deficiency. The largest heather garden which I constructed covered an acre of ground and included a stream with pools. The smallest, an island bed measuring 20 ft by 10 ft (6 by 3 metres), carried an interesting selection of mini-*Calluna* and *Erica* providing a most efficient insect foraging place. The resident dunnock spent a lot of daylight hours there as well.

I have already mentioned the various forms of *Juniperus x media* there are; others in the juniper family which are absolutely prostrate, with ornamental foliage. A pool edged with *Juniperus squamata*

109

The Joy of Wildlife Gardening

'Blue Carpet' and *J. horizontalis* 'Glauca' combined with the golden foliaged *Juniperus squamata* 'Hodges' is effective all the year round, forming a good weed-suppressing, living mulch. *Tsuga canadensis* 'Cole' is like a green waterfall if given a boulder to grow over, and a form of *Picea pungens* called 'Kosteri' makes a burnished silver carpet just a path width away.

There are some beguiling forms of our native yew (*Taxus*) which form quite effective ground cover. I grow *Taxus baccata* 'Dovastoni Aurea', 'Cavendishii', 'Repens Aurea', and several more. Nearly all are females and berry freely – which makes them an especially valuable food source.

Consider also the innumerable forms of ivy (*Hedera helix*) as ground cover in shade, under trees, over banks and similar inhospitable places. A mixture of plain and variegated leaved forms underplanted with snowdrops and winter aconite leaves no room for criticism or weeds.

The long border which faces north and is completely shaded by the house except for long periods in high summer is largely given over to dwarf *Rhododendrons*. None have grown more than a yard high in the ten years since they were planted. Foliage interest is, of course, year round, and the flowers add another dimension to the word profuse. There are three *Rhododendrons* in this border I would consider 'must haves': 'Elizabeth' with scarlet blossoms in May produces a fugitive show again in autumn, 'Blue Diamond' is as the name suggests, and is most free-flowering, while 'yakushimanum' is excellent in all things – in shape, leaf, and flower. They grow in a humus-rich soil along with snake's head fritillary, snowdrops, lilies, primroses, violets, and other woodlanders in an harmonious community. The dense canopy of foliage and peat mulched soil offer a feeding place to dunnock, wren, robin, and the blackbirds when the open garden is frost bound. Indeed, the blackbirds have curious ideas about mulching – no sooner have I spread compost on the border soil than they redistribute it across the lawn. A shade border is a bug rich, slug abounding and worm-infested hunting ground for a whole range of garden life – bird, hedgehog, vole, mole and even the occasional weasel. The border takes possibly three hours of my labour each year to maintain, and is good to look at even in mid-winter.

Cotoneaster dammeri is always included in lists of plants which make effective ground cover. In my experience of three gardens where *Cotoneaster dammeri* was planted, the foliage blanket is *not* sufficiently dense, and hand weeding between the branches took hours of time. Now I use *Cotoneaster dammeri* oversown with *Limnanthes douglasii*, a delightful annual with cream and yellow flowers. This really is a useful combination; just as the bees finish working the *Cotoneaster* flowers, the *Limnanthes* comes into bloom and continues into September when the *Crocus speciosus* pushes up deep lavender goblets. As a last contribution, the *Cotoneaster* offers berries to foraging blackbirds.

Cotoneaster microphyllus thymifolius is also meritorious. I grow it with herb Robert and *Saxifraga oppositifolia* as an edging to the rock wall. The saxifrage is a most welcome first glimpse of spring, the ruby red flowers are usually evident sometime in February. The *Coton-*

ALPINES

Ajuga reptans (Bugle) in variety – 4 in (10 cm). Shades of blue. May – June.

Alyssum saxatalis varieties. 10 in (25 cm). Yellow – spring.

Armeria caespitosa and **maritima** varieties. 3-9 in (6–15 cm). Cushion forming, pink to red – spring.

Aubrieta Any of the single flowered varieties. 3-8 in (8-20 cm). Mat formers, various colours – spring.

Campanula (Bell flowers) Any alpine species or varieties 5-12 in (12-30 cm). Indispensible. Blue, purple, white – summer.

Dianthus (Pinks) Any of the alpine species or varieties. 3-10 in (6-25 cm). Pink, red – summer.

Geranium Any of those offered in alpine lists 4-8 in (10–20 cm). Red, pink – all summer.

The wren is one of our commonest birds, but its stealthy habits make it quite hard to see. Watch your ground cover plants and low shrubs carefully: there you are likely to find a little wren busily searching for spiders and other insects. Wrens rarely come to bird tables, so try throwing a little grated cheese around your garden's borders instead.

Helianthemum (Rock Roses) 8-13 in (20-30 cm). Quick growing ground cover shrubs, various bright coloured flowers – summer.

Hypericum coris 6 in (15 cm). Yellow – all summer.

Iberis 'Snowflake' (Candytuft) 10 in (25 cm). Shrublet. May – June.

Phlox douglasii and **subulata** varieties. 4-6 in (10-15 cm). White, pink, red, or blue. May – June.

Primula All dwarf forms including Primroses and those needing moist conditions. 4-24 in (12-60 cm).

Sedum Varieties of *floriferum*, *spathulifolium*, and *spurium*. 4 in (10 cm). All mat formers. Pink, red, or yellow – summer.

Veronicum prostrata varieties 4 in (10 cm). Blue, purple, and pink. June – August.

Viola (Pansy). For long flowering – any listed under alpines in seed or plant catalogues.

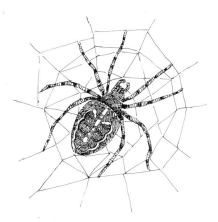

The most obvious spider is the garden spider, its beautiful, regular web is a familiar sight.

easter/herb Robert mixture blends into the carpet of mixed *Ajuga* with variegated leaves and spikes of blue flowers which are searched for diligently by insects.

Ground cover plants are not confined to those of prostrate habit, a part of the border which is almost completely self maintaining is planted with shrubs and herbaceous plants. There is a narrow leaved laurel, *Prunus laurocerasus* 'Schipkaensis' which having changed gardens three times with me, actually packs its roots each time a furniture van passes. No weeds compete with this flat-topped, darkly evergreen bush which is bone hardy and flowers profusely at a different time every year (which confuses me if not the bees). The spikes of white flowers 8 inches (20 cm) long smell like almond kernels. The purple-black berries must be eaten by bird or beast, for they rarely survive long. Fronting the laurel, *Euphorbia polychroma* whose yellow flowers in late April help bridge the east wind hungry gap. A mixed lot of *Hosta*, *Epimedium*, and as a solace for summers passing, hardy *Fuchsia* continue in flower to November. I am surprised each year how often bees and other insects are found feeding on the flowers in mid-October. Not surprising really for even as my pen scribbles this down three swallows are hawking low above the lawn, and a glance at the calendar declares the date is 15 October.

Hebe once enjoyed a reputation for being tender. Indeed, some of them are too sensitive to survive in this garden, despite encouragement. Others are excellent value for garden decoration and as providers of forage flowers and cover. There is a most enormous bush of *Hebe brachysiphon* a metre high by two metres broad which I planted on a herb garden wall. When covered in white flowers during June and July it attracts every bee and hoverfly in the parish. Indeed, this bush forms a centre piece to one of those garden cameos which are partly contrived and part happy accident. The retaining wall supporting the herb border is matted with a tapestry of thyme whose flowers range in colour from pink to dark red. Combine this with silver-grey cotton, lavender (*Santolina*) and a *Berberis* with dark red foliage called *B. thunbergii* 'Erecta', and the effect can be imagined. I almost forgot the angel's fishing rod, *Dierama*, which though buried under the *Hebe*, still pushes up slender stems hung with pink bell flowers. My wife and daughter consider this the best part of the garden, so do the wild birds, for it is where I put out their winter food. Wife and daughter join in eating outdoors in summer, then move inside for the winter!

Let no-one be persuaded into believing that ground cover plants are for the big garden scene only. Some of the most useful carpeting plants can be found amongst the alpines. I have a *Cotoneaster hybridus* 'Pendulus' which is grown on a short stem then spreads out as a green carpet over the surrounding soil. This is the centre piece of a tapestry of *Aubrieta*, *Phlox douglasii*, and *P. subulata*, with *Sedum floriferum* and *spurium* throwing in their quota to the floral display. This combination would make a complete suburban wildlife garden. The *Cotoneaster* flowers and berries more abundantly than almost any other shrub I know – so makes a long term food source. Then the *Aubrieta* starts a flowering succession which continues from April to November. The cheddar pink is also part of the package, all mixed up

Ground cover plants: *Juniper pfitzeraria*, **ivy, dwarf rhododendron (Elizabeth),** *Cotoneaster hydrophyllus* **'Thymifolius',** *Euphorbia polychroma, Epimedium, Fuchsia, Santolina, Taxus, Berberis thunbergii* **'Erecta',** *Aubrieta, Viburnum opulus* **'Compactum', herb Robert.**

with *Campanula* so there is no lack of fragrance.

Shrubs which are dwarf and useful because they flower, berry, and have weed-inhibiting foliage, must deserve a mention. The guelder rose grows too large for inclusion in the modest plot, except that is, for the dwarf form – *Viburnum opulus* 'Compactum' which combines well with *Berberis* 'Green Carpet', and *Euonymus fortunei* 'Emerald Gaiety'. The *Viburnum* grows to a metre high and the typical white lace cap flowers are followed by a handsome show of glistening red fruits. The *Berberis*, slightly dwarfer, also flowers then fruits as the leaves turn brilliant scarlet during October. The 15 inch (38 cm) tall *Euonymus* provides year round interest with white and green leaves. While cleaning up the garden near this group of shrubs last autumn, I found a greenfinch's nest full of *Berberis* and *Pyracantha* berries in the beech hedge, so there was no need to print a menu of what is on offer.

By the skilful use of shrubs, herbaceous plants, and annuals the time-consuming work of weeding can be appreciably reduced. There are those who dwell rapturously on the pleasure derived from hand weeding – I am not so afflicted. There are so many more interesting things to do in a garden, like leaning on a hoe in contemplation, or sitting on the well edge counting the number of forays a dragonfly makes, that weeding comes very low down on my list of hobbies.

Peter Rowe

15. Autumn's brief magnificence

Of all the seasons, autumn is my favourite; the profligate season which spreads her largesse abroad in one dramatic gesture. Its influence is apparent everywhere, from the moors, always the first to show bronze then fox red, to the copse furrowing along the hedgerows before the dying leaves strike their colours in surrender to winter. Sunlight now is softer, muted, yet of just the quality to bring out all the subtle cadences and colour tones. I catch myself pausing just to listen, for it is as if the countryside were encapsulated in a timeless silence that is so essential a part of the season.

There are moments which transcend the mere description of beauty. Sunlight filters through a shower of pale gold larch needles which add to the carpet already shed, deadening our footsteps so we are at one with the all-pervading quiet. And there are mornings when trees, shrubs and flowers are all laced together by cobwebs jewelled with mist droplets, and the *Dahlia* border glows iridescent as sunlight breaks through the morning mist to light the flowers.

There are moments also when the sad finality of the season touches me closely. Swallows still hawking over the garden in mid October, a flickering echo of summer soon to be gone. It is important there should be flowers in the garden to attract the insects for those late hatched youngsters to feed on, enabling them to build up good reserves for the long journey ahead.

Make sure too that drifts of leaves are left to accumulate at hedge bottoms, or better still over a pile of pea rods placed for that very purpose in a sheltered corner. There the hedgehogs, those imperturbable slug-eating gardeners' aids, will find a secure retreat for the winter. A little contrived untidiness is essential if the garden is to play a full part in the conservation pattern. Left until spring, the stems of herbaceous plants provide a foraging place and short term cover. And tits, wrens, dunnocks, and goldfinches will make good use of any untrimmed border.

Anyone with a large garden might consider growing ornamental thistle, giant hogweed, and teasel which make a most handsome jungle of stems with first insect-infested flower heads for birds to feed on, followed in the autumn by a crop of seeds. Though the hogweed can cause dermatitis if handled in hot weather, providing it is properly sited there is no more useful forage plant to be grown from seed. The flower head carried on a nine foot (three metre) high stem measures six feet (two metres) across like a great white umbrella. When in bloom the flowers are a crawling mass of midge-like insects of which small birds are not slow to take advantage. One of the best

Grey squirrel – active in autumn looking for acorns and chestnuts. It also raids birdtables!

The Joy of Wildlife Gardening

reasons for growing the giant Scotch thistle *Onopordum acanthium*, apart from the silver-grey foliage and purple flowers, is that it attracts goldfinches to the garden as the seed ripens. The silver, geometric outline of the thistle etched against the blue wash of an autumn sky, with a charm of goldfinches practising high bar gymnastics as they feed on the seed, forms a picture so pleasing that the prospect of approaching winter is almost bearable.

One of the pleasurable and at the same time frustrating pursuits which I look forward to each autumn, is fungus hunting. Toadstools are a vital part of the countryside survival pattern. They break down leaf litter, rotting wood and vegetation, then when they die, they release the stored nutrients back into the soil for re-use by other flora and fauna. Toadstools and mushrooms are also a food source in themselves. Squirrels hunt for *Boletus* and others with almost the same enthusiasm as the Ukrainians who taught me what little I know about cooking toadstools. I was well schooled on the subject of mushrooms, from childhood, and still get the same keen pleasure from early morning expeditions across quiet fields in search of those mysterious white buttons. That many toadstools are ornamental is obvious to those who have seen the scarlet, white spotted caps of fly agaric pushing up through a golden litter of birch leaves: a small, grey slug feeds on this fungus, poisonous to us, and thrives. So even when toadstools invade the lawn I do not reach immediately for the fungicide, preferring to watch the squirrels snatch a meal *en route* to the oak trees just a lane's width away.

The oak tree should perhaps be classified as a habitat in itself, for one well grown specimen supports an incredibly rich and varied lot of wildlife. There are galls on leaves, and caterpillars and aphids feed a host of insect-eating birds, wasps, flies, and mammals. In the autumn of a good acorn year, the scenes of gluttony verge on the disgusting. Wood pigeons, rooks, jays, magpies, pheasants, squirrels and mice all compete with others un-namable except by those better informed than me, for a share of the bounty. As a child, I used to gather bags full of acorns and feed them to the pigs whose gluttony and table manners made those of an eight-year-old boy seem almost acceptable.

Autumn is also the time of change in an even broader sense. The feverish activity is a compulsive act of survival, a storing up of reserves against the bleak days ahead. A hedgehog, after a last shuffling exploration under the crab apple, retires to a snug retreat. Swallows, house martins, and other migrants have left to be passed *en route* by an invasion of fieldfares, redwings, and most stimulating of all to the imagination, geese. So often when making a last check round in the crisp brightness of autumn moonlight, the sound of a conversational passage of geese overhead has lifted my spirit. For a fleeting moment, I shared company with the truly blithe spirits of this world and was richer for that experience.

There is also opportunity to express a gathering instinct, latent inside even the most sophisticated microwave owning, pre-packaged food-conscious and centrally heated house dweller, to gather in stores for the winter the bounty of woodland and hedgerow. One such pleasure is gathering blackberries on warm afternoons: there is

N G Blake (Bruce Coleman Ltd)

116

E A Janes (Nature Photographers)

(Left) Fly agaric is an instantly recognised fungus, found with birch trees. Autumn is enlivened by the sudden appearance of mushrooms and toadstools – the fruiting bodies of fungi working unseen below the ground.

(Above) Autumn fruits such as blackberries provide a feast for birds and late summer insects, like this red admiral butterfly. For apple and pear trees, to reduce the risk of disease to the parent plant, gather any unwanted fallen fruit and put it down elsewhere, rather than let it rot in situ.

some urgency to harvest them before they are touched by frost and become 'the devil's property. Another is picking crab apples and rowan berries to be turned into that amber-coloured jelly that matches so perfectly the taste of freshly baked scones. Always there is the underlying compulsion to store, provoked by the uncertainty of whether our unpredictable climate will allow sufficient time to save, store, and enjoy all that autumn has to offer.

Only recently I had an example of this very waywardness of the season. I had been up on the moors and was following a green lane down between dry stone walls. To one side on millstone grit lay peat-encrusted moorland with heather and bracken – a glory of bronze and gold. To the other, the gentle and friendly undulations of lime-stone, all patterns of grey on bright green. In the ghylls, rowan, hawthorn, and wild cherry in full scarlet, orange and copper leafage made the contrast between the two views even more stark. As I cut across to Skyreholme, the wind lifted, clouds rolled in and shafts of sunlight briefly transformed loveliness to ethereal beauty that made me pause in wonder. Only for a few brief moments was the picture held before I was enveloped in a hailstorm of unbelievable ferocity. Crouched behind the doubtful shelter of a wall I reflected on the contrast between my present situation and the ecstasy of the moment before. These rapid changes are what makes autumn so compelling. Like a wayward child first smiling, then tearful, pensive, and in an instant passionately wanton. All I can say is that those who garden enjoy the season more than most.

117

16. Bees hum among the herbs

Make your garden practical as well as beautiful: fresh herbs will enrich meals, they are easy to grow and insects love them!

Herbs can make a marvellous feature in any garden, whether as the dominant area, or grown in a small patch or even tubs. Make for easy access to the back door so that they can easily be gathered when wanted.

A herb garden is more than just a collection of plants which are useful and decorative. Rosemary, lavender and madonna lily are a living link with the ancient civilizations who explored by trial and error the uses of plants both as food, and for their medicinal value. The ancient laws of the apothecary were once lost but are now being rediscovered and used in modern medicine. Add decorative qualities to herbs' prime uses as food and in medicine, their further merit in wildlife terms, and they achieve a well deserved pre-eminence.

There is one herb garden which for many years I visited regularly in spring, summer, autumn, and winter that would serve as a standard pattern. The long, narrow borders sheltered by yew hedges led to a summer house surrounded by roses which were notable for their scent. Even on the coldest day this corner of the garden offered a refuge from wind and weather. There was, I remember, a sundial set in a cobblestone circle carpeted with thyme which found root hold amongst the earth-filled crevices. The summer house offered a changing pattern of plants which were too tender to survive outdoors and spent the winter in a frost-free greenhouse. Lemon-scented *Verbena* and scented leaved *Pelargonium* were herbs only in the sense that they were used in pot-pourri.

A herb garden needs to be both secluded and sheltered with a soil which is free-draining and faces due south. My host surprised me one day with the comment that any gardener from Pliny down through the centuries would be immediately at home in a herb garden. As Pliny wrote on botany during the 1st century AD, my surprise at the remark is understandable. On thinking back, botanists, wise women, monks and apothecaries would be familiar with and have better understanding of the uses of most of the herbs we grow today than I possess.

Most garden-worthy herbs have their origins in a much drier and warmer climate, the Mediterranean being the natural home of many aromatic plants which grace gardening in Britain. By constructing a herb garden we share in a common experience with those who invented the names of herbs we now use. Lovage, gilly flower, mignonette, pellitory of the wall, and sweet cicely roll so naturally off the tongue as to erode time and make a yesterday of centuries.

Though herbs will coexist quite happily in the rough and tumble of the open garden I prefer to give them a corner to themselves. On warm evenings, to sit quietly and enjoy the compendium of scents is a most pleasurable experience. Let me assure those with a very small plot that there is no need to devote precious growing space in the

Most herbs prefer a well drained soil.

garden to herbs – though they are as worthy as any of consideration. Even with space available in my existing herb border I still plant a choice selection in containers on the terrace. I grew the most fragrant sorts in tubs, troughs, and a window box in the cobbled yard at the back of my grandparents' house. In spite of being in shade for a considerable part of the day, in retrospect and with more experience, I am astonished at how well they grew.

Herbs are so determinedly informal that even when planted in rigidly geometrical beds they express an undisciplined look which is endearingly reminiscent of a cottage garden. Given this characteristic, herbs are suited by whatever convenience the garden affords. Straight rows across the vegetable plot, a corner near the back door, or even the grand conceit of a knot garden, their unique quality will pay an abundant ground rent on many a bee-busy, butterfly haunted summer afternoon.

There are those who argue that herbs growing wild are found in every soil type from weeping bog to shifting sand, and all degrees of light or shade. I remain unconvinced that any site will do after trying to make a herb garden on heavy clay where only the coarse survived. On poorly drained soils raise the herb bed above the general level, or grow a selection of the choicest in tubs. For only in a sun baked position and a well drained soil will herbs distil the fragrance which is their prime virtue. There is a need also for a seat close by. In my garden the retaining wall of the herb garden is raised to a comfortable sitting position height, and is so well upholstered with a carpet of thyme as to be acceptable to the most lightly covered posterior.

Sorting out the best herbs to grow is made a little easier by the qualification that they must also be attractive to wildlife. I remember growing comfrey, possibly the most efficacious of all herbs, for the goats which for years added a new dimension of pleasurable exasperation to my life. They resolutely refused to eat a single leaf, so I used it as green manure for growing peas and potatoes – a most effective way of improving poor soil. The flowers which are borne in July and August are variously coloured purple, pink, and white. This was one of the herbs that grew well in the clay soil. In an Italian garden I visited when researching the history of the *Iris pallida*, a source of orris root, comfrey grew abundantly. There the scarlet tiger moth caterpillars almost defoliated the plants. Those living in southern England should look for their brightly coloured black and yellow caterpillars; in the north I have so far looked in vain.

Both yarrow and *Ajuga* are old fashioned wound herbs and deserve a place with comfrey as a plant of healing: that bees feed on them voraciously is a further recommendation. *Angelica* is a plant handsome enough and sufficiently interesting to warrant inclusion. For centuries it has been used for candying, and in medicine. The large rounded umbels of greeny white flowers are attractive to insects, and birds feed on these during nesting time.

Lungwort, the 'soldiers and sailors' flowers of childhood, with curiously spotted lung-shaped leaves and two-toned flowers in shades of blue and pink, is much frequented by flower bees. At first glance the flower bee looks like an insect version of a jet-propelled, hovering bumble bee. Flower bees have long tongues which enable

The Joy of Wildlife Gardening

them to exploit tubular flowers like those of the lungwort, jasmine, and primrose.

There is a very sound, practical purpose in grouping plants which flower early and are attractive to insects in a sheltered corner close to a shrub border or hedge. I have noticed whitethroats and spotted flycatchers seek such insect-thronged places, even to the extent of choosing a suitably placed perch. The bowed top of Young's weeping birch is one which the birds use here as a base from which to dart out and seize insects. The various essentials – plants, insects, and suitable hiding places – were all topped off when the ivy planted five years ago provided enough cover on a dry stone wall to serve as a nest site. The warblers, also summer visitors, work more from the seclusion of an overgrown copse just a lane's width away.

There must be balm – as there was in Gilead – for the bees take such a voracious interest in the small white flowers, and the lemon-scented leaves offer a refreshing fragrance. A tea made with balm leaves and sweetened with honey, is a drink to savour.

So many herbs are attractive to butterflies. Marjoram is aptly named 'Mountain Joy', if the Greek *Origanum* is literally translated *oros* (mountain) and *ganos* (joy). In Tudor times, marjoram was grown in knot beds where the purple and white flowers were used in nose-gays. Possibly because marjoram and hyssop were always linked in ancient garden lore I allowed them to share a corner in my herb garden. The blue flowers of hyssop are attractive to butterflies and pay a pretty compliment to those of the marjoram. I have also noticed that lacewings, those voracious eaters of greenfly, are frequently in evidence about the taller growing herbs. The value of lacewings as a biological control of greenfly in organic gardening is often under-estimated. Lacewings have a delicate beauty of their own: green bodies and gossamer wings veined with pale lime colour suggest that they are nectar-sipping rather than flesh-eating insects. The larvae suck the juice from aphids much as we drink soda water through a straw, while the adults adopt the more direct method of crunching aphids and other small insects as if they were fleshy potato crisps.

Lavender, rosemary, and thyme are plants of such quality that cuttings made from the original herb garden plantings are now spread around the garden. A bush of lavender by a much-used path is kept pruned by passing fingers nipping sprigs of leaves, or blue flowers when in season in order to make a closer appraisal of the delectable scent.

Ros marinus dew of the sea is the wild plant of Corsica and Sardinia we know as rosemary, most beloved of herbs. Certainly few herbs carry such a long historical pedigree or have proved so useful in medicine, cosmetics, or kitchen. In the garden of a house which I had a long association with for almost a year, rosemary covered the whole of a hot dry earth-filled wall and bees seemed to harbour there even when the plant was not in bloom. When the blue flowers appeared in May to June butterflies, hoverflies and a host of others joined the conversationally busy bustling bees. Grow rosemary, herb of remembrance, in a sheltered corner where the evergreen foliage will be least at risk from frost discolouration.

My first experience with thyme should have ensured that I would

HERBS

Angelica archangelica (Angelica) Perennial 5 ft (1.5 m). Tall greenish-white flowers – July to August. Excellent insect forage plant.

Melissa officinalis (Balm) Perennial 3 ft (90 cm). Tall white flowers – July to August.

Laurus nobilis (Bay) Evergreen shrub, bearing small clustered yellow flowers in June, followed by fleshy berries. For insects, birds and cooks. Tender in some areas.

Borago officinalis (Borage) Annual 2 ft (65 cm) high. Sky-blue flowers over a long period. A valuable bee plant.

Anthemis nobilis (Chamomile) Prostrate perennial. White, yellow-centred flowers during July and August.

Allium schoenoprasum (Chives) A hardy bulbous perennial 6 in (15 cm) tall, with pink and blue flowers. August – September. A butterfly and bee plant.

Hoverflies are often mistaken for wasps, but their 'thick waists' give them away. To us they are harmless, but they are welcome predators on aphids both in the adult and larval stages.

Foeniculum vulgare (Fennel) Perennial 4ft (1 m) in height. Umbels of yellow flowers during mid-summer attract myriads of small insects which birds feed on.

Lavandula angustifolia (Lavender) Shrub 2 ft (60 cm) tall. Blue flowers are in evidence during summer from July onwards.

Origanum vulgare (Marjoram) Perennial 12 in (30 cm) tall. Flowers rosy-purple during late summer.

Mentha (Mint) In various forms make good herb garden plants. In good soil tends to be invasive.

Rosmarinus officinalis Rosemary Evergreen shrub up to 6 ft 6 in (2 m). Blue flowers in May make a valuable early nectar source for bees and others.

Thymus (Thyme) All species are useful for bees and butterflies to forage on. They are shrubby perennials which vary in height from 3-12 in (7-30 cm).

Bees find the herb garden particularly attractive. The flowers of chives, mint, lavender, rosemary, hyssop and borage act as a magnet.

never wish to grow the plant again. As a young gardener I was given charge of a lawn made from thyme which had to be hand-weeded while kneeling on a board. The episcopalian lawn as it was referred to in polite circles enjoyed many a more lurid description from me. During the course of long, hot summer days spent picking annual meadow grass, dandelion and other weeds from a matted carpet of multi-hued flowers, I invented a whole catalogue of titles both for thyme lawns and those who had the things planted. In spite of such early rancorous encounters my affection for thyme, both as garden decoration and herb, remains undiminished. Several forms of *Thymus drucei* planted along the low wall have masked it completely, and the tapestry of different coloured flowers in summer is lovely. There are those with golden leaves, the *T. citriodorus* 'Aureum' is one I grow in the herb garden proper, along with others which smell of camphor, citrus or even carroway seed. I can heartily recommend making a collection of thyme as a pleasant, rewarding pursuit. Then watching and identifying the different sorts of insects which gather to feed on the flowers makes a welcome alternative to working on a hot summer's day, for thyme, like so many herbs, flowers better and is more discernibly fragrant in drought conditions when other plants are wilting.

Sage and southern wood I grow for my own pleasure rather than that of the itinerant population. I plant lovage, and fennel behind them as they do in Tuscany, just as an apology for self-indulgence. Both these umbellifers grow quite tall, from three to four feet on average and when in flower, they tempt every passing insect to wallow in the gelatinous droplets of nectar. Borage also shares a corner with this group and its brilliant blue flowers are eagerly sought after by bumble bees who have great difficulty in plundering the downward facing nectaries.

Mint there must be for the small magpie moth in particular to feed on, and to ensure the leg of lamb is correctly dressed for dinner. Mint I would put in the same class as *Sedum* in the butterfly attracting table, though not quite to the extent of Michaelmas daisy and *Buddleia*. I grow 'Apple Mint' for my wife who is addicted to mint sauce with everything. All others, 'Eau de Cologne', 'ginger', 'pineapple', 'lemon' and 'peppermint', are grown for the outdoor staff, namely me and the other insects. Tiny, creeping pennyroyal, and the Corsican *requienii* are shade tolerant and so I grow them in the shade border where they produce an abundance of minute, purple flowers for the butterflies to test-taste. Mint will spread far and wide over the herb garden given the opportunity, so I keep it suitably confined in polythene sleeves. These are made from compost bags cut in half then buried in soil where they are completely invisible, yet prevent the mint roots growing beyond their prescribed bounds.

One of the surprising discoveries made during experiments with plants in relation to wildlife is the value of most onion flowers as insect attractors. *Allium*, to give their collective botanical surname, be they culinary or merely ornamental, are worth growing for the butterflies alone which feed on the flower heads. The flower clusters come in various shades of pink, purple, red and yellow, with white thrown in for good measure. If forced to select two I would choose yellow-

Harry Smith Horticultural Collection

G D Smith

Rosemary, mint and thyme are among the most useful of culinary herbs, while attracting all sorts of insects. There is a superstition that rosemary should always be given and never bought! There are several types of mint, some hardier than others. Ordinary garden mint can be quite invasive – grow it in a pot, or contain its roots in a bucket or tub sunk into the earth. Thyme – several types are available, lemon thyme is a golden-leaved variety – grow it in full sun. Most herbs need sunny, well drained positions in order to thrive.

flowered *Allium moly* for early flowering and *A. sphaerocephalum* with dark red blossom. Butterflies, moths, and various bees contest and jostle for a turn at nectar guzzling. Grow orache, the beautiful red-leaved 'mountain spinach' mixed up with *Allium* with its purple seed heads. They look well together and the nutmeg moth will regard it as a personal favour.

Grow parsley and asparagus, not just as cooking aids, although that is, of course, an essential priority. Allow some of the plants to grow flower heads and ripen seed. Insects, particularly the ladybirds and cardinal beetles, seem to favour the open canopy flower heads.

I also make room for hogweed and sweet cicely for the ginger red soldier beetles use both plants as dining room and mating area. As the seed ripens, insect-eating birds are replaced by seed eaters. I like to grow wide-canopied plants with lace-patterned flower heads along with shrub roses; I add a few meadow crane's-bill as well to make an attractive garden feature.

The boundary wall of my first garden was a natural garden in itself, and it was here that I first saw pellitory of the wall, red valerian, and even lavender growing between crevices in the stonework. It was there that I also gained a more intimate acquaintance with red osmia bees which gather pollen using the bristle-like hairs on the undersides of their abdomen. The crevices of this wall filled only loosely with a mixture of earth and lime mortar, were a hiding place for wolf and other spiders, and innumerable insects which wrens could be seen feeding on at any hour of daylight all year round. Pied wagtails divided their time equally between lawn and wall. The walls in my present garden serve a similar purpose though not so efficiently.

The Anglo-Saxon woodruff is no more than a modest little creeping perennial with insignificant heads of small white flowers which open in springtime. Hummingbird hawkmoths feed on other members of the clan, so I ask myself, why not on this little frequenter of hedgerows and woodlands? I have another reason for reserving a place for woodruff in a lightly shaded corner. A sprig pulled and hung up to dry in my work place exudes the distinctive sweet scent of new-mown hay, as will sweet vernal grass when first cut. Self indulgence again I admit, though for the sake of a few seeds scattered amongst the herb Robert at a path edge I can wallow in nostalgic memories of haytime during those magical years of childhood in the Dales. There is also the prospect of watching hummingbird hawkmoths demonstrate their fascinating skill of hovering and feeding simultaneously.

17. 'All nature was degraded' – or all muck can be magically transformed

Make your own compost: it does your plants good and the animals like it too!

There is a lane leading from the village across the green to what was once, in the days of my youth, the village school. The full two hundred yards (200 m) or so of its rough cobbled length were overhung by trees including beech, oak, and an enormous horse-chestnut. At the school end stood two wild cherries whose leaves rivalled those of the horse-chestnut in their brilliance of autumn colour. The fallen leaves piled in drifts knee deep to a child, and each autumn I waded through them inhaling the spicy aroma before rain and trampling feet reduced them to a flat, decaying uniformity. Later on in my life, I gathered the mixed beech and oak leafmould from those same trees to mix with loam and sand as a basis for potting compost. Thinking back, this was my first introduction to composting. In much the same careless way my early years in gardening ingrained in me a commitment to organic principles which neither college training nor chemical propaganda have swayed.

If the greenhouse is the heart of the garden, then organic matter is the life blood and compost the haemoglobin. There is no better way of improving the all-round condition of soil, drainage, moisture retention and ease of working than by regular feeding with compost or manure.

Many years ago I took upon myself the task of making a vegetable garden on a glacial clay soil. The farmer who had the land prior to my renting it was less than encouraging. Each time he passed my ear was bent with stories of cows sinking up to their bellies in muck every time it rained. The list of crops which had failed there, including turnips, was beyond recollection. After seven years I could dig the vegetable plot with a shovel and it would grow any vegetable including the best asparagus I have ever tasted. There was no magic about how the transformation came about – just three compost bins in a corner of the garden. As for the farmer, his comment rendered me speechless, 'all that land needed was a strong back and a weak head!'

A healthy soil means more than just good crops. Regular dressings of organic matter encourages vigorous and abundant populations of worms, bugs, bacteria, and fungi. Birds, animals and others feed on these so adding the final piece to complete the gardening with wild-life jigsaw.

126

There is deep satisfaction in turning what is generally classed as rubbish into a material which is so exceedingly beneficial to garden soil. Years ago I had a contract with the greengrocer in a town six miles away to remove all moribund fruit and vegetables. I persuaded a neighbour who worked in the town to bring all the decaying vegetation back three evenings a week in exchange for a regular supply of fresh fruit and vegetables. Mixed with lawn mowings, straw and herbaceous litter it made compost of a very high quality. From then on I have composted almost anything which will rot down and be of use in the garden. Spent hops, cotton seed waste, shoddy and even leather shavings and barber's shop sweepings were all grist to the compost mill. I was actually paid to remove the enormous heaps of sawdust which had built up to be an outsize nuisance at the local sawmill. Mixed with stable manure, they took two years to rot down, yet when used as a mulch on blackcurrants the compost stimulated them into producing strings of fruit like black Hamburg grapes.

The composting process, even in summer, is not something to be rushed. Work on the principle that one heap is better than none, two is a distinct improvement, while three makes an abundance. The bacteria which break down all dead vegetation, including that heaped into the compost bins, need much the same conditions as we do to function. They need air, moisture, warmth and in the initial stages of breaking down the raw material, food in the form of nitrogen. They cannot function efficiently if acid builds up during the decay process, so a dusting of lime is not only good insurance but rather more a necessity.

My compost bins are made from wooden slats 4 ft (1·2 m) long nailed to uprights, and spaced an inch (2·5 cm) apart to permit good air circulation. This produces bins four foot square (1·2 × 1·2 m) and four foot six inches (1·4 m) high of a handy size to fill quickly. Though some people resolutely maintain that a compost heap will swallow any organic material and regurgitate it as good compost, I am more selective.

Never introduce seeding weeds or the roots of pernicious perennials such as dock, bindweed, couch, creeping buttercup, ground elder (well named the bishop's curse), or nettles into the bins. But let me qualify the last named by saying that nettles minus the roots and mixed with comfrey and straw make the best composts of all.

Avoid also diseased or pest-ridden material, cooked kitchen waste, potato haulms, and very woody prunings such as rose, unless they have been pulverised in a shredder. I also shred things like windfall apples, turnips, brassica stalks, newspapers and old woollens before adding them to the heap. Fallen leaves are best kept in a heap on their own.

Fill each bin quickly so that heat – an essential part of the composting process – builds up rapidly and is then maintained. I work to my own composting routine established after years of trial and error experimentation. The bins stand on soil, and I always leave a shovel or two of made compost as a starter. During the lawn mowing season I keep a bale or two of straw to mix in with the mountains of grass clippings. This prevents them sogging down into an airless, putrefying heap. Straw is to bacteria what bran is to a well-balanced human diet,

My compost bins are made from wooden slats.

Roger Hosking

or so it appears to me. Apart from this I just pile the compostable vegetation in as it comes to hand. For every 15 inches (38 cm) of depth dust with lime, alternating with a nitrogen activator. I keep both in a watertight container alongside the bins to make certain they are used in proper rotation.

Once a bin is filled I cover the open top with a piece of old carpet. This works as a protection against excessive moisture on the one hand, while conserving heat and moisture on the other.

Animal manure – horse or bovine – applied to the soil is a traditional method of improving fertility. Because fold yard litter from beasts bedded on straw is readily available I use it for mulching every square yard of my soil which is very light and dries out quickly. I also keep several barrow loads for worms and bacteria to break down into

Denizens of the compost heap include hedgehogs and bank voles. The hedgehog will find a plentiful supply of worms, slugs and insects.

128

that black brown material the more erudite describe as humus. All gardeners, as one comedian put it, need a sense of humus.

Litter from horses bedded on shavings will break down much quicker if a high nitrogen activator is mixed in with it during the bin-filling process. All manure heaps should be covered with a polythene sheet to protect them from weathering. Do leave the sides open so the mass can breathe and not become a suppurating, noxious smelling, putrefied heap.

Let anyone who doubts the value of mulching, try covering a part of the shrub border as an experiment. The birds, particularly blackbirds spend hours turning the mulching material over in search of food. I spend hours in consequence raking litter from lawns and paths back onto the soil where it belongs. There is a knock-on effect, the blackbird using its beak like a mattock disturbs the mulch and takes first pick. A robin observes all this herculean labour from a convenient perch close by. Once the blackbird moves on, or sometimes before, the robin moves in to take a share, and dunnock, wren, and thrush will also explore the disturbed litter, because the humus-rich moistness harbours a variety of life including slugs, worms, beetles, mites, springtails, eelworms and a host of other beaksome or toothsome delights.

Loose mulch gives cover for shrews, voles, and other animals, while in the shadier, moister areas I have found frogs, toads, newts, and on one memorable occasion, a grass snake. Unfortunately, my mother found the snake first when picking rhubarb and did not share in my excitement or linger to be introduced.

Butterflies will sometimes busy themselves in fallen litter where their folded wings, like dried leaves, are excellent camouflage. This is why I leave most leaves to rot where they fall, only raking up those from the lawn onto the shrub borders. To keep them in place I throw shovelfuls of sand on top of them.

A layer of leaves or a rough mulch of compost or farm manure makes a useful winter refuge for some hibernators. Do not be alarmed if toadstools grow on the mulch. They are a visible sign of the secret process of the breakdown of organic matter which is going on all the time. Otherwise the accumulation of litter would bury house, garden, and gardener. Just to illustrate the point, over a ton of litter per acre falls each year in some deciduous woodlands. Fungi help re-cycle this so that the nutrients become available for the green plants to use over and over again.

Even before the compost is spread about the garden, the heap, being warm, attracts bumble bees and grass snakes to nest there. Toads will also over winter in the snug, moist warmth and in hard winters wrens spend time searching the accessible parts of the heap. Dismantling therefore requires due care – give the robin time to investigate every forkful and you will not disturb a clutch of snake eggs, or stab a slumbering common lizard.

18. 'Fruit for their songs' – or fair shares for all!

Luscious vegetables and fruit can be grown alongside rather than in competition with the birds and caterpillars

Research has shown that the density of blackbirds is higher in residential areas than in the open countryside. I could have proved that true by my own experience as a 17-year-old. Part of my duty in those far off halcyon days of youth was to check the netted fruit each morning during summer to make certain no birds had broken through the barrier. In those pre-plastic days nets were made from cotton or twine and the birds searched every inch for a sign of weakness. In their efforts to get at the fruit they became hopelessly tangled in the net and had to be cut free. Strawberries, raspberries, cherries and plums were all covered, and in terms of tantalising succulence, cherries appeared to rank top in the birds' palatability list. Fortunately modern plastic nets do not offer a similar hazard to birds or animals.

Ventilators in greenhouses had to be wired against squirrels which scrambled through any gap large enough. The damage done by squirrels to peaches, figs and nectarines once inside the greenhouse was unbelievable. Instead of finishing one fruit the beasts went around nipping pieces out of dozens.

The same competition for who had what share was evident in the vegetable garden. Pheasants, pigeons, rabbits, hares, roe deer, and on several occasions badger were uninvited guests. I never did succeed in fencing out the badgers yet kept them at bay by soaking their trail into the garden with a noxious smelling liquid which kept both badgers and everyone else up-wind of the place.

A well stocked orchard and vegetable garden is compatible with a thriving wildlife population, providing it is based on the principle of fair shares for all. A word of warning: domestic pets are not above being seduced by fresh fruit and vegetables. My daughter's tortoise had to be banned from the garden at strawberry time such was the reptile's passion for the ripe fruit. My last dog, so special there will never be another, helped herself to ripe tomatoes from the greenhouse; carrots, and of all things Brussels sprouts from the garden. That she also scoffed every blackcurrant within neck stretch earned her a detention on many a summer day.

Lizards living in the dry stone walls used to lie sunning themselves, catching spiders, greenfly and anything else edible which could be seized with minimum effort. I was almost certain, though could never prove it, that one portly lizard that inhabited a crack in the stoke hole wall, ate the cabbage-white butterfly caterpillars. Again, though unable to prove it, I am sure it spat out the skins. As I was supposed to be fully occupied hand weeding frames at the time, my wildlife studies had to be conducted surreptitiously.

Net the strawberries and other soft fruit to keep out birds, but make sure the net is well above the plants and taut, or you might witness an interesting trampolining act on the part of determined blackbird! Slugs can be deterred from vulnerable plants by covering the surrounding area with a little soot or bark mulch. A slug trap using beer as the bait will not harm other creatures.

One of the most notable contributions to garden wildlife was in the form of cultivated blackberries which included varieties specially selected from wild plants the head gardener found in nearby woods and hedgerows. The number of butterflies and moths in addition to a variety of insects attracted to the flowers makes the lowly bramble a most useful forage plant. Green hairstreak, gate keeper and hedge brown butterflies, grass eggar and fox moths, and the quite extraordinary spectacle of the night flying emperor moth abroad in daylight were all identified feeding on the bramble hedge during my six years tenure of the garden. Unlike so many fruiting shrubs, the blackberry is in bloom over several months until early December according to my observations. The rich and succulent purple fruits attract man, bird, beast, and insect to share in the harvest. Wasps extract the rich juices in a final gourmet feast before they are killed by frost. I have also seen red admirals and speckled wood butterflies about the bushes though they have been exploring the flowers. Blue tits search for the larvae which hatch from eggs laid in the flower buds months previously. Blackbirds and other seed eaters pillage the fruit, while any which fall to the ground are gleaned by bank vole and wood mouse. Foxes enjoy a dessert of blackberries as do squirrels, and as a nesting site the tangled stems of blackberries is accommodation of the four star class.

After working for six years in the all organic garden I left to attend college where everything that did not move was either sprayed or painted, and the *Silent Spring* forecast by Rachel Carson almost became reality. Nowhere was the contrast between the ancient and modern more stark than in orchards. In the one, lichen-covered trees were given only minimal spraying and feeding although they were carefully pruned. But trees in the commercial college orchard were sprayed every week and four times monthly, as an Irish friend of mine put it. The warning to wash or peel any 'scrumped' apples before eating them was most timely, for the spray used against sawfly was extremely poisonous. To someone accustomed to the pick and eat before the head gardener catches you principle, this was extraordinary.

Chaffinches nested in the crook of an apple tree branch somewhere in the unsprayed orchard nearly every spring. The nest was a lichen, moss and cobweb structure so camouflaged as to be almost undetectable. Bullfinches and tits demolished the blossom buds on fruit trees and growth buds on the gooseberries. Imitation hawks and quassia sprays were used to persuade the birds to go elsewhere. Windfall apples provided pickings for birds, wasps, bluebottles and hedgehogs amongst others. In the college orchard, all windfalls were gathered for burning in case they harboured sawfly, codlin or the disfiguring apple scab.

Fruit will need protecting of course, or the gardener would hardly manage to taste any in competition with birds that begin foraging at dawn. Any fruit unfit for presentation at table can be scattered outside the net as a solace to frustrated non-human scrumpers.

You hardly need to be a fanatic dedicated to self-sufficiency to realise that a carrot pulled from the garden, then wiped clean on a trouser leg or skirt and eaten tastes better than the same article from

Wasps enjoy the sweet fruits of autumn. They can damage apples and pears that are on the tree, but generally are homing in on damage caused by other creatures first.

The Joy of Wildlife Gardening

a polythene bag. Lettuce has a crispness and flavour which only slugs enjoy unless you grow salads no more than ten strides from the kitchen table. I noticed years ago when conducting trials on lettuce how the birds always chose the best flavoured. From a dozen popular varieties the sparrows always plundered 'Buttercrunch' which happened to be my own choice also. I discouraged them from eating 'Buttercrunch' with wire netting cloches, so they ate 'Trocadero Improved' instead.

An intensively cultivated vegetable garden does not make ideal wildlife habitat, but given a little well-considered neglect it can, however, be improved. Mulching down rows of long standing crops like Brussels sprouts, protects soil against compaction and provides a hunting place for wrens and dunnocks which is safe from predators. I plant crops close together and the dense canopy of foliage prevents the soil freezing in hard weather – to the advantage of blackbird and song thrush. Close planting does not reduce crop productivity.

Digging empty ground is one of those jobs ideally suited to a cold day and which affords me immense satisfaction. To my eye, the clean, weed-free expanse of fresh turned earth is a thing of beauty. Always one and sometimes several robins accompany the work with quarrelsome competition. Blackbirds search the freshly turned soil for worms, and when worms are scarce, rooks drop in from the rookery only 50 yards (54 m) away. I make a point of covering part of the vegetable plot in straw so when the soil elsewhere is frost-bound, digging over the mulched part is still possible – a piece of forethought which keeps me in work and provides for the birds.

This is not a theoretical projection of a re-constituted pre-apple tasting Eden where all was harmony. A vegetable and fruit garden *is* a practical possibility without using sprays which present a threat to wildlife. Moles can be and indeed are a nuisance in lawn or vegetable plot. They are permanent residents in my garden but somehow the plants still thrive in spite of being undermined. Have a certain sympathy for the mole; after all, I find digging hard work, and from above, with a spade. The mole has to toil from below with only bare paws. To deter moles, all I do is mix up one of the animal deterrents that gives off a stench which moles detest, and pour that into the subterranean runs. This is not based on the principle of love your neighbour I admit, for the offending mole merely moves next door to untainted territory!

Strict hygiene is a basic tenet of orchard and vegetable garden cultivation, particularly in regard to pest and disease control. I would not argue with this for it is, after all, common sense. But there are compromises which are not dangerously permissive. A heap of prunings raked up and left in a corner over winter will suit hedgehog, mouse, vole, and several different kinds of 'creepy-crawlies'. In due course it can be cleared away long before the dread plagues which the heap might harbour spread to infect the whole garden.

By grouping overwintering crops in a rough garden-cum-habitat rotation the vegetable garden becomes much less of a predator's paradise by providing cover for feeding bird and beast. I strip off the leaves of sprouts, broccoli, and kale, and let them lie where they fall as a green mulch. Then at intervals they can be roughed over with a wire

Most gardeners have a 'tame' robin that puts in an appearance as soon as the spade is wielded. The simple confidence of this small bird must be one of the most rewarding experiences of gardening.

Ardea

Robins can find desirable residences in discarded watering cans, kettles and flower pots; vindication of the less than perfectly tidy gardener perhaps! Leave a window of the potting shed slightly open (not wide enough to admit a cat) and one or two plant pots or other receptacles on their side.

rake or fork to reveal all the juicy tit-bits as a snack for birds with courage enough to sit out winter with us.

Over the years I have seen some quite remarkable examples of adaptability on the part of the fauna which are permanent garden residents. One robin moved into the greenhouse via a broken ventilation hole each evening just at dusk. In due course this bird became so tame that it perched on the bench watching me prick out seedling cauliflowers and bridge grafting pears. There was a toad which spent the summer near the water tank in a tomato house, and all winter underneath a rhubarb-forcing bench. This one rejoiced in the name of Reilly, whose life he was surely living!

One winter I had the task of clearing a large orchard then preparing the ground for vegetable crops. The fire I started to get rid of stumps and twiggy pieces too small for logs, burned for six weeks through the vicious winter of 1963. A wren, normally a shy bird, never moved from the immediate vicinity of the fire, feeding all the time on insects disturbed by the heat. When all else was bound iron hard with frost and buried under snow, this feathered entrepreneur lived a cosy, centrally heated existence to the extent of roosting in a root-tangled stump protected from the inferno for me to sit on during meal breaks. The plot of ground I cleared grew crops of vegetables except where the fire had been. Apparently the concentration of salts and depletion of humus in the soil, far from encouraging growth, actually depressed it.

One thing I have proved umpteen times is that given a modicum of tolerant understanding on our part, wildlife is quite prepared to meet us half way. But it does not prevent me from rushing out to net the winter greens against marauding 'stockies' – a local name for wood-pigeon.

G D Smith

Winter comes and the wildlife watching gardener is in his element!

19. 'Winter, Frosty but kindly'

Each season has a positive identity with characteristics peculiarly its own. The rolling call of a curlew echoing across the dale means spring is abroad in the land. Swallows holding conversation over the possibilities offered by the garage as a suitable nesting site holds all summers gentleness in a few brief phrases. The smell of *chrysanthemums*, sharply acrid, and the crowing of a cockerel loud on the still mist-hung air of late afternoon can only be a product of October. What then is winter? Apprehension that the weather may prove again the utter futility of man's inventiveness, with frost and blizzards of snow. Not really, for winter affords moments of beauty so fragile as to make them all the more memorable. A tracery of branches etched against the duck egg green and pale orange sunset. Picture holly, the loveliest of evergreens, with red berries rimmed with frost. The birds busily feeding on nut dispensers and on the bird table form a living cameo of a real world as opposed to the flickering artificiality of television. Or a walk out into the star studded darkness, the quiet so intense one can almost hear the squeak of a world revolving on its axis.

I would hate to live in a country where the seasons were not clearly defined. Not that they are here, for January frequently offers a taste of spring. Winter is a time when we can enjoy a closer, more intimate contact with birds which find sanctuary and hospitality in the garden. The force of hunger almost equals the mating instinct in its compelling intensity, blunting the edge of fear. Of the 25 different sorts of birds which are regular visitors to my garden in winter, none are so tame as the robin and blackbird. I consider money spent on bird food a very good investment which is always repaid with interest. To watch the great spotted woodpecker trying to monopolise two nut dispensers spaced 15 ft (3·2 metres) apart offers a comic picture of frustrated greed which never fails to entertain.

Silver birch I would have planted anyway, in the cherished hope that long-tailed tits would accept the invitation it offered. This year they did and seven avian acrobats searched every twig and bark crevice only a short distance above my head, all the more satisfying because I grew the trees from seed.

Winter reveals what was hidden during summer. How could I possibly have missed the greenfinch's nest almost under my nose in the shade border. The nest is now full of winter's debris and probably only recently housed the greenfinches feeding on the holly tree nut dispenser.

As birds gather closer to the house hard pressed by a prolonged

The Joy of Wildlife Gardening

frost we have the opportunity to discover each as an individual. One male blackbird full of confidence comes up to my feet as I put out the twice daily feed while another stays under the hedge until I am back indoors. I have had blue tits settle to feed while the container was being filled within fingertip distance. One evening I counted 14 blue tits going to roost in a hole in the garage wall. They must have slept snugly piled one on top of the other.

The first fall of snow reveals a tale of what trafficking to and fro went on under cover of darkness. A wood mouse's tracks leading to almost 30 yards (27 metres) across the lawn to where the first *Crocus* were showing yellow shoots through the soil before being blanketed with drifting snow. What thoughts, if any, of marauding owls or foxes crossed its mind as hunger overcame fear? The marks of a tawny owl's pounce were clearly defined by the print of its outstretched wings on the back lawn. Mice treck out from the dry-stone wall to feed on nut and corn remnants, and owls soon discover the place to be – a well stocked 'game' reserve if corn-fed mice are game enough.

A fox makes a routine inspection of the bird feeding places, his or her line of ruler straight tracks clearly recorded in the snow. I had to change the position of two half coconut shells filled with a suet-based mixture, as the fox somehow managed to reach and eat the contents.

As Christmas approaches, the attempts and strategies invented by my family to preserve just a few holly berries to use as decoration become even more frantically aggressive. The flapping of tea towels, waving arms, and muttered expletives are now a familiar part of the festive season. Being the only Scrooge in the family I prefer holly berries on the bush and pine trees snow dusted against the ice blue sky of winter, but never indoors. Now if crossbills feeding on the pine cones were included as part of the indoor decoration then I might suddenly be converted by the ghost of Christmas yet to come.

There is, of course, work to be done in the garden including digging compost or manure into all parts of the vegetable plot not under crop. Pruning fruit trees is another dormant season job. The flower borders I leave untrimmed, for there is a beauty in rime-frosted russet and bronze. Even lovelier are the goldfinches and on one memorable occasion the siskin which came to feed on the seed heads. Amongst the better known seed bearers, teasel, thistle, sunflowers and *Astilbe* are popular feeding places with blue tits and finches.

No sooner has the old year been tolled out and the new year launched – or drowned – according to your perspective, than the pace of life quickens. Snowdrops, hardy *Cyclamen*, witch hazel and the fragrant winter blooming *Viburnum* gladden the short hours of daylight. It is surprising also how many hovering, dancing gnats are evident on warm days. By the time *Aconites* spread their deep yellow under the pale primrose blooms of *Mahonia*, the hive bees are about their business. At first they are seen only briefly, at noon on mild days as robin, blackbird and tree sparrow begin sparring matches on the frost-burned grass.

The rooks paired off weeks ago, as did the partridges, regular visitors to the garden until lengthening days lighted the procreative spark. Both rook and partridge share with curlew and plover a special niche in my affection. To see a great conversation of rooks returning

Feeding birds can be of real benefit to them during hard weather, and what more cheering sight than a blue tit's acrobatics on a bag of nuts?

in the gathering dusk is a joyous event; a twisting, tumbling frollicking, garrulous concourse of mischievous fun. The partridge churring down the field edge and pecking daintily at spilled corn on the lawn will in a month or two be leading its newly hatched young to feast on ants by the lane verge – a model of parenthood.

I grow willow and hazel in the garden because the lambs' tails of one and the pussy catkins of the other are a portent of spring, more reassuring perhaps than the first primrose. Important also that bees should have an alternative pollen source if mice have eaten all the *Crocus*, and willows are reliably excellent in flowering early. The more adventurous butterflies, persuaded out of hibernation by several warm days in succession, also need a reliable source of energy-rich nectar.

Under the hedge bordering the copse dog violets and *Celandines* are in flower by late February. Nettles also push up early growth – the young tips cooked briefly in boiling water have a flavour more delicate than spinach. The nettle is such an important food and fodder plant for red admiral and painted lady butterflies, and scarlet tiger moth, and in spite of the latter's marked preference for comfrey, I only take a modest share for my own use.

Last December there was the quite extraordinary sight of a skewbald stoat, pure white except for two brown patches and a black tip, hunting the dry-stone wall bordering the garden. As there had been no snow I could only assume the animal cherished a secret ambition to become part of some judge's accoutrements!

Very early in the new year I begin sowing seeds in the greenhouse. I start with annuals, especially the half hardy sort which require a longer sowing season than our summer affords. Some vegetables also need to be given an early start: peas, broad beans, cauliflowers, and onions profit from being grown under glass then transferred outdoors in late April. Walking across to the copse for a fresh supply of compost I noticed that the green shoots of hedge mustard I planted for the convenience of green-veined white butterflies are sprouting forth. The blackbird practises a few stanzas from a perch on the greenhouse roof, and I am reminded that all the lime deposits from previous visits will need cleaning off. Growing plants require all the light a grey February affords. I must also shovel snow from the birds' feeding ground, replenish water in frozen containers, and melt a hole in the ice covering the pond. Winter is far from dreary.

Some butterflies hibernate. Look for small tortoiseshells secreted amongst the rafters of your garden shed.

A variety of garden bird equipment is available from the RSPB: nestboxes, birdtables and hanging feeders will all help to attract birds to your garden.

20. Send out an invitation (Come into my garden!)

Nestboxes and birdtables

The shortening days which herald the approach of winter do limit the number of hours during which birds and animals are able to forage for food. Just after 4 pm on Christmas day our holly tree blackbird is safely gone to roost. The blue tits may linger a few minutes longer on the nut dispensers, catching the last of the sparse afterglow before they disperse, some to a cavity wall, others to the nesting-boxes which in spring were the connubial couch.

To compound the problem faced by all wildlife in winter there is also the seasonal decline in the supply of natural food. The struggle for survival is on, and as winter spreads searching fingers to discover any weakness, so the beleaguered birds and animals become more dependent on our hospitality. I for one am delighted this should be so, for in winter it is possible to become more intimately acquainted with birds in a way that is not possible during the easy going days of summer and autumn. As hunger, that persuader against fear, exerts full authority, so even the most shy birds draw closer to share in the food provided. This is a time when the nuts and crumbs put on the windowsill by those who have no garden can perform a life-saving service.

The giving on my part is not altogether selfless. Watching birds and animals busily feeding has been one of winter's anticipated pleasures ever since as a small boy, I scattered hen corn and hung up marrow bones. To those who have never shared the experience I would merely say that a well stocked bird-table is both entertaining and educational. Certainly it is a most acceptable alternative to hibernation.

The bird feeding ground needs to be open, yet sheltered from the weather, and with good cover close at hand. Having watched a sparrowhawk which regularly hunts the area casually pick a blue tit leaving the nut dispenser, I can appreciate how important a handy sanctuary is for feeding birds. Some birds are reluctant to feed anywhere else except on the ground, so I scatter some of the food, particularly mixed corn, on the lawn. Searching for the grains encourages a natural behaviour pattern which adds to the pleasure and interest of watching. Fruit which includes apples, pears, and anything else the season offers, is also best placed on the ground. What a blackbird makes of a sudden appearance of apples in mid-winter baffles my imagination. Birds tend to be fastidiously particular in the matter of diet, except for magpies, starlings, and others whose crops, bearing in mind what is stuffed into them, must closely resemble coffee grinders. By observation it is easy to discover which bird likes what food. I experiment all the time with mixed corn, peanuts, suet, mixed wild bird seed and fruit as the basic daily diet. Because I am fortunate in having pheasant and partridge visit the garden a little grit is added to the corn.

Make certain there is a drinking place near at hand. I use two stones which I put into the pond to give birds a safe drinking place. A large plant saucer 18 inch diameter by 2 inches deep (46×5 cm) plunged to rim level on the back lawn suffices as a second water hole. Birds not only need to drink, but they also need to bathe regularly to keep insulating feathers functioning efficiently. To see a blackbird sloshing around in the drinking bowl on a bitter cold day, then sitting and preening himself on the holly tree adds a new dimension to the old adage 'cleanliness is next to godliness'.

A bird table can be of any design, but there should be a raised edge all round to prevent the food being shot over the edge by flapping wings and skidding feet. Some birds will be content to feed on the ground. That lovable little gleaner, the dunnock, is often busily engaged seeking crumbs, like Lazarus, around the base of the table. What a selective feeder the dunnock is even in hard weather, so I make special provision for this self-effacing bird. In many town gardens, one of the regular attenders at the bird table is the grey squirrel which is not, I must admit, on my top twenty list of animals. A few strips of the grease banding used for apple trees, or a saucer collar round the pole will deter this predatory creature.

Mice, foxes, stoats and weasels are all potential visitors to the bird feeding station. Unfortunately, so also are rats which quickly discover almost any source of freely available food. One of the most interesting examples of natural predation has on three occasions been enacted here, or at least began near the bird table. On the last occasion of stoat versus rat, the *coup de grâce* took place almost at my feet just outside the shed door. Each time, in a last desperate effort to avoid being killed, the rat turned onto its back to protect the vulnerable nape of the neck where the stoat takes its killing hold. Mice come for the corn; owls, stoats, weasels, and even foxes come for the rodents, so the table can be a feeding ground for all.

Having safely carried the birds through winter into spring, I like to persuade them to take up a permanent residence by putting up nesting-boxes in strategic places. One point which should always be borne in mind is the comfort of a bird brooding eggs, and in course of time, that of the nestlings.

Never place a nesting facility so it faces due south because the inside of a box in full sun gets very hot, and in most cases birds ignore it anyway. The Royal Society for the Protection of Birds produces an easy to follow, step by step instruction leaflet on how to build nest-boxes of all shapes and sizes which even the least able handyman should have no difficulty in following.

There are so many alternatives to the standard wooden box with an entrance hole provided that I am convinced birds are the great improvisors. Who would imagine a blackbird choosing to nest in the top of the left foot of a pair of Wellingtons hanging up in an open-fronted tool shed. It was fortunate indeed for a robin which built in the top of a soil sterilizer, that the seed-sowing and potting season

Nestboxes and birdtables can be made quite easily. Careful siting of both is important however: away from predators and in the case of nestboxes out of direct sunlight.

had just ended. Pieces of wood pushed in behind wall plants can make useful nestboxes. A clay land drainage tile performs a similar function. The most popular nesting/roosting places in this garden are the holes left when the garage was being built. Ten days after the final roof slate was laid, blue tits were building in the first hole.

Birds need to bathe regularly, at least, some of them do, and not just in summer. I have watched starlings, blackbirds and sparrows bathe in late afternoon on distinctly chilly days and wondered if this cleansing of the plumage improved insulation. In the absence of a pool of any sort, put out bowls of water, or better still, provide a bird bath. Birds at their ablutions and preening offer an interesting example of meticulous care, and the ability to get at the parts even a certain alcoholic beverage couldn't reach!

It is no use providing everything birds, animals, and other wildlife need if the garden is not first, last and at all times a safe sanctuary. Do everything possible to ensure that the only thing they have to fear is natural predation. This means non-interference, but I make an exception of cats, because no matter how well-fed, they have a hunter-killer instinct. To thwart the numerous felines which patrol my garden I keep a high-powered hosepipe ever-ready. Cats hate cold water liberally applied and the hunter soon becomes the hunted.

Food for birds can include: breadcrumbs, cake, raisins, grated cheese, fat, suet, nuts, coconut (not desiccated), mealworms, seeds, bacon rind (chopped). Try making a bird pudding – melt some fat and pour it into a mould. Place a string inside so that as the fat hardens you will have something to hang it up by. Add nuts and crumbs and other suitable scraps, leave the fat to set, then hang the 'pudding' on a tree or your birdtable.

B Gadsley (RSPB)

21. Garden chemicals and how to avoid them

The amount of thought and creative energy expended in the design and construction of a wildlife garden is considerable. Time and patience will be needed while the maturation process takes place. Until a reasonably stable maturity emerges from the intense competition going on all the time in a natural environment, I try to be a merely passive though keenly interested observer.

This is not so difficult, for experience has shown me that such a balance is possible. Good crops can be grown without constant recourse to sprays and dusts. In the private garden where my basic practical gardening training took place, top quality fruit, vegetables and flowers were required all year round. A limited amount of damage from pest or disease was acceptable as part of the price to be paid for not using massive amounts of chemicals to control aphids, red spider, scab and other unwelcome intruders. I have observed the principles and practices of gardening learned in those first six years right through to the present day. What I find so remarkable is that it has taken so long for the chemical revolution to be called into question.

Just one example will suffice: in the 60 acre (20 hectares) garden that was in my care for 20 years, I picked up a sackful of dead and dying birds after a neighbouring farmer had sprayed fields of arable crops. They were mostly rooks, a few starlings, three pheasants, and one partridge. I never did find out the spray used or for what purpose. One effect of this traumatic experience was to strengthen my determination to question in practical experiment any spray or dusts termed 'safe' before recommending them to anyone for use.

The fruit and vegetable garden offers the best environment for a build up of pest or disease until they reach epidemic proportions. Moving the different crops around the plot is a sensible, though not totally effective measure. To spread the fungus causing club root of cabbage all about the garden only needs a clod of infected soil sticking to a boot. Rotation certainly uses the fertility of a soil in the best possible way, for crops vary in the mineral elements which are essential for healthy balanced growth. A cabbage for example, being a leaf vegetable, requires extra nitrogen as this encourages quick, luxuriant growth. On the other hand carrots are a root crop so are given phosphates as a means of promoting well flavoured roots. This is the best argument in favour of rotation, that by so adjusting each year's crops, full consideration is given to their nutritional needs. There may be the additional bonus of pest and disease control.

Let there be no doubt that taking into account the cost of tools,

What could be more rewarding than swallows nesting near your home? Along with our other summer migrant birds, they eat vast numbers of flying insects, reason enough for avoiding chemical control of insect pests.

143

The Joy of Wildlife Gardening

seeds, land and labour, home grown produce costs more in real terms than those bought from a supermarket. Home grown vegetables and fruit are fresher and of better flavour and there are no hidden additives or chemical residues of the dusts and sprays used in commercial food production to control pests and diseases.

There *are* simple ways to prevent plague and pestilence ravaging crops. I also enlist the aid of the natural predators which devour greenfly or relish cutworms wherever possible. Cabbage root fly I have had no trouble with; the problem is resolved by slipping a square of felt or carpet underlay of dimensions 4×4 inches around the stem at soil level. Make a slit into the centre, with a small cross slit at the end to accommodate the stem. The felt prevents the cabbage root fly from laying eggs in close proximity to the stem and not a plant will be harmed.

A disease of the cabbage family, called clubroot, can remain alive in the soil for many years. All I try to do is provide conditions which better suit the cabbage than the disease. First I give the soil a very heavy liming, for the fungus causing clubroot prefers acidity to alkalinity, so score one for the gardener. Then I raise all my own stock of cabbage, cauliflowers, sprouts, wallflowers and any other members of the cabbage clan from seed. Buying plants in is to run the risk of bringing the infection with them. The seedlings are grown on in pots made of peat or similar material so that when the time comes for them to be planted out they are well enough advanced to, at least, produce a modest crop.

Potato blight can ruin a whole season's work by making the tubers unfit for storing. Bordeaux mixture sprayed at fortnightly intervals from mid-summer on will harm nothing except the disease.

A fence of polythene two feet high (half a metre) all round the carrot bed will stop carrot root fly gaining access. The fly homes in, attracted by the smell of the foliage, hits the screen and flies up to clear the obstacle and right over the bed altogether. I put a dusting of soot down between the rows to kill the smell of carrot which attracts the fly in the first place. During winter a fold unit with bantam chickens can be put on the vegetable plot, each day the unit is moved onto a strip which has had the top three inches (eight cm) of soil lightly pricked over with a fork. The cutworm, carrot fly, or anything else which escapes their careful scrutiny would need to be a master of camouflage. Failing bantams, keep the soil of the vegetable plot well cultivated to give garden birds easy access to soil-borne nasties.

Pests the size of caterpillars are big enough to hand pick, at least those which are not eaten by birds, lizards, or parasitised by ichneumon flies which lay eggs inside their victims. One with the unlovely name *Cocygomimus* lays its eggs in cabbage-white butterfly caterpillars. They hunt mainly at night, selecting their prey by scent. Just stand in the garden with a torch and the slender-bodied ichneumons will come to dance in the beam. Aphids, the ever-present greenfly, breed at such a phenomenal rate it is our good fortune that they are food for so many of our garden residents. Many birds rely on greenfly for readily available food for nestlings. Ladybirds, both adults and the bluish-coloured larvae which look like crocodiles, chew up the greenfly in surprising quantities. Indeed, the larvae of ladybird are

Protect young cabbage plants against cabbage root fly with a layer of felt underlay.

possessed of such an insatiable appetite they will bite chunks out of each other just to keep their jaws in practice.

Wasps certainly do more good than harm in the garden so should be for the most part encouraged. Having several times shared a slice of bread and jam with wasps during picnics outdoors I would suggest the word 'encourage', can be taken too literally. The most important are the social variety as opposed to the digger wasp. Social wasps are similar to bees in forming colonies, and they feed their young on masticated caterpillar, greenfly, and other insects. On a diet like that I would feel a distinct inclination to sting something, although wasps do not use stings to paralyse their prey. Like the tiger they so much resemble in colour, wasps have very strong jaws used to seize their victims. One of the marks of stinging insects is this vivid colouring – a sort of 'hands off I'm dangerous' form of self defence. Some hoverflies found about the garden have adopted the striking black and yellow pattern which is a form of protective mimicry. Young birds, which, like the rest of us learn by trial and error, soon discover that insects with black and yellow stripes usually sting if pecked. One or two experimental pecks are sufficient to drive the lesson home and thereafter wasps and hoverflies are left off the menu. The main damage done by wasps in the garden is to ripening fruit. A few jam jars filled three quarters full with beer should solve the problem. Like some gardeners, I have known wasps to prefer ale to apples.

The same technique works with slugs – a saucer of beer buried to the rim near vulnerable plants will keep slugs happily occupied all night instead of chewing lettuce. To drown in best bitter must be far preferable to being de-slimed with slug pellets, and less dangerous to other wildlife. A word of warning; my neighbour's dog, and even a hedgehog family discovered the beer-baited slug traps. The dog became addicted to his liquor straight and emptied the saucers almost quicker than I could fill them. That hedgehogs prefer slugs pickled in home brew to the untainted sort I can vouch for as fact. A possible explanation could be that an intoxicated slug is easier to catch. Purpose-built saucers are pet proof, only slugs can get at the beer.

Several of the pests which attack fruit trees can be a problem, yet not one which is insoluble. The chickens and geese which had free run of the orchard at home must have accounted for a lot of potential fruit pests. All I can remember is the satisfaction felt when the enormous Rhode Island red cockerel which had attacked me at every opportunity, was almost flattened by a ripe 'Peasgoods Nonsuch' apple which fell on him.

Grease bands were always fitted round the trunks of apple trees each autumn to trap the wingless female moths when they crawled up to lay their eggs during the winter.

Usually the first sign of codling moth is half a maggot left in the apple I have just taken a bite out of. This is, I agree, one method of control if someone else can be persuaded to do the biting! Female moths produce a chemical to attract the male and scientists have succeeded in manufacturing this. A dab of the 'love potion' inside a trap lined with sticky paper accounts for a good number of male moths, leaving a similar number of females unproductive.

Sawflies also cause serious damage, particularly to gooseberries.

The little owl feeds largely on worms, insects and other invertebrates. It was introduced to England during the 19th Century as a controller of garden pests.

The Joy of Wildlife Gardening

Unless controlled, they can completely defoliate the bushes and reduce the crop of berries by 75 per cent in epidemic years. Birds will deplete the caterpillar numbers, particularly when feeding nestlings. The robins and tits treat sawfly caterpillars as a dainty main course. Just to help out, for birds do not take enough sawfly to prevent serious damage to the bushes, I spray with an insecticide made from a mixture of derris and pyrethrum, and then net the bushes. Though the spray will not harm adult birds I take no risks where nestlings are concerned.

In cultivated soil, leather-jackets (the larval stage of daddy-long-legs) need not be a pest. By keeping the soil tilled, the larvae are exposed to view and birds feast upon them with obvious relish. Leather-jackets can be a major pest in a lawn by feeding on the grass roots. And in August and September clouds of craneflies festoon walls, bushes and the lawn. A female can lay up to three hundred eggs, so from that, estimate the number of larvae feeding on the grass roots and it is not surprising that damage to the turf can be so serious that dead patches develop. Pied wagtails, like high speed clockwork toys, scurry around catching the adult craneflies. Mostly they hunt on foot, but frequently make little aerial forays, more a jump than actual flight, to snatch an insect out of the air. For entertainment value a pair of foraging wagtails takes some beating, which is why they are in my top ten bird list.

The ground beetle is another quick moving predator which will eat leather jackets, wireworms, slugs, and most other things classified as pests by the gardener. Though they prefer hunting at night there is one very high powered member of the clan frequently to be seen sunbathing on the limestone rock garden near the pool. The name of this particular effete beetle is so suggestive of gluttony as to be almost libellous – *Notiophilus biguttatus*. I presume and hope the 'big-guttatus' is due to an over-indulgence in slugs! Ground beetles flourish in large numbers where there is plenty of shelter under low growing shrubs or ground cover plants. I encourage them even further by laying flat stones or pieces of hessian for them to co-habit under.

Wireworms, those pests of newly cultivated pasture, are larvae of the click beetle, so not all things beetle shaped are friendly. When in doubt, before using the 'heavy boot' insecticide, tip the beetle over onto its back. A click beetle rights itself with a most acrobatic and audible snap of, presumably, its thorax – in which case it can be given the ancient order of the hob-nailed boot. My present garden was made out of a field which had been pasture since ancient Britons roamed the land and the wireworm population was phenomenal. They ate carrots, potatoes and any other plant root which was offered, even to the extent of nibbling my boot soles if I stood still long enough. I reduced the infestation to negligible proportions by repeatedly cultivating the soil. The local starling population only had to see me take digging fork in hand and they were sitting on the wall waiting. Burying pieces of carrot, turnip, and potato tubers will attract wireworms to them – the traps should be removed at intervals and shaken out on the bird table – the robins think they are sun-burned mealy worms and eat them with relish.

Pied wagtails turn into aerobats as they try to snatch craneflies from the air.

Garden chemicals and how to avoid them

Cutworms are another subterranean pest which live just below the soil surface. They are the caterpillars of moths belonging to the family *Noctuidae* with over 20,000 species worldwide, so swatting even on a large scale is out of the question. Fortunately not all the noctuids are pests in the garden, though with each female laying up to 1,000 eggs in a fortnight this is small consolation. Heart and dart, yellow underwing, garden swift and ghost swift moths are the most common and most infamous. Fortunately, birds regard cutworms as a delicacy – my pet rook almost got trodden on during winter digging in her eagerness to inspect each spadeful. Ground beetles will also search them out and the grubs are easy to see so can be hand picked when exposed by routine cultivations.

For most of the problems described as pests there is a natural control: lacewings, ladybirds, hoverflies and of course birds, will all destroy greenfly. The frogs and toads which make themselves free of the garden and use the pond as a connubial couch, will eat lots of small insects and slugs. Hedgehogs will, or so it seems to me, chew anything which ventures near, cutworms and slugs especially, though a crunchy beetle, woodlouse, or wireworm also serves as *hors d' oeuvre* and main course. I reward the labouring hedgehog with a spoonful of cat food in hard times.

Centipedes are splendid, fast moving predators that feed on insects, slugs and, let truth be told, worms as well. Given adequate cover, low growing vegetation, stones, and seed trays left on the garden over the weekend, the centipede population will flourish to the gardener's advantage.

The harvestmen, those *Arachnids* which so closely resemble spiders, except they have a one piece instead of a two-piece body are very desirable aids, feeding almost entirely on a wide range of bothersome bugs and beetles. To see a harvestman examining a caterpillar before making a meal of it is to witness an exercise in fastidious gluttony. First the gravy splashing feast, then the wash and brush up, for to be successful a harvestman needs to have limbs and above all a keen sense of smell, unimpaired.

I am convinced that encouraging birds to centre on the garden by putting out food for them during the winter is a major factor in keeping pests within acceptable bounds. In between stuffing themselves on nuts, suet, and anything else on the *table d' hôte* they forage vigorously about in the trees and shrubs looking for more natural food. Tits are particularly valuable in this respect, also the treecreeper and great spotted woodpecker that are regular winter visitors. Starlings may be bird-table guzzlers, yet do spend time investigating the lawn for leatherjackets, wireworms, and who knows what delicacy to the avian eye.

The mole, which at times I condemn nose, paws, and velvet texture to the nether regions, must in the course of 24 hours of tunnelling account for creatures that would do much damage to my plants.

When worried by pest or disease in the garden, I console myself with the old adage, 'for every problem under the sun there's a remedy or there's none; if there is, try and find it, if there isn't, never mind it'.

The Joy of Wildlife Gardening

Frans Daalen

22. Specific problems – the snake in your Eden!

When adopting the principle of 'open house', or in this case, garden, some of the co-habitors which move in will, on occasion, become a nuisance. This is not a breaking of rules for there are none except those we contrive and apply. For the wildlife garden to be a mirror image of the wilderness, there should be the minimum of interference on our part. After all, the mole which in one frenzied night of sub-terranean activity ruins the lawn with a series of mini-Everests, is behaving naturally. The grey heron which periodically raids the pond for goldfish is merely another bird, albeit with expensive taste, taking its share of what we have provided along with the other wildlife. Indeed, I am flattered that so many truly wild creatures accept my garden so readily as a sanctuary. This in no way prevents me getting hopping mad when the last golden orf disappears down the heron's rapacious maw. But I do not in consequence declare war on herons. Rather, I merely make fishing a little harder.

The very act of making a pond, then stocking it with fish, is almost like issuing an open invitation to fish-eating birds. We might just as well put out bags of peanuts and not expect blue tits to come and eat them. Circumventing the angling heron is not difficult. Constructing the pond in such a way that there is no gradually sloping shallow area to give easy access for the heron is the best and most effective deterrent. Anyone who has watched herons will have noted they prefer not to drop direct into the water. A bird intent on feeding settles first on the bank, then after a careful survey steps into deeper water like some fastidious debutante testing the temperature. My present pool is edged with weathered limestone, and so, try as they will (and do regularly), no heron has yet tasted one of the fish. I repeat however wildlife ponds function best devoid of ornamental fish and with sloping sides.

Small pools can be netted, while large areas of water can often be protected by putting an 18-24 inch (45-60 cms) wire fence round. Herons are birds towards which, over long years of association, I have developed a sympathetic understanding. My first job after leaving boarding school was four miles (6·5 km) from home. I had to cycle to work each morning following a narrow, lonely track, leaving home before dawn. The lane, for it was no more than that, crossed seven streams in the four miles, and always on two of the becks there was a heron standing in exactly the same place every single morning. Indeed, one of the earliest memories of those early morning rides is of a grey shape poised motionless by a tumbling rock-strewn stream. So the heron is synonymous in my mind with wild, lonely places, such as

Deter herons by placing a wire around the edge of your pond.

149

The Joy of Wildlife Gardening

Scargill, Kilnsey, Hickling Broad and Garnish Island; a creature happy with its own company, a strand in the web of the countryside.

Moles I am slowly learning to live with, except in lawn and vegetable plot, for elsewhere they appear to do little harm. My garden is absolutely riddled with runs and so are those of my neighbours, one of whom trapped 17 moles in a half-acre (0·25 hectare) plot in one year. To keep them out of lawn and other no-go areas I use a metal rod – once a fire iron – to find the runs, then push rags soaked in renardine or scoot into them. This, as one neighbour points out, merely sends them next door – so I offered him the can and rod to do likewise. One garden guru advised de-worming the lawn, which removes the moles' food supply and so the reason for doing any burrowing. The same guru then buys expensive equipment and spends hours making holes to relieve surface compaction of the lawn which the worms did for him for nothing. Watching the tug of war between a hungry thrush and a large worm determinedly resisting being turned into breakfast, is something the owner of the wormless lawn will never have appreciated. So, for the benefits derived from their sometimes annoying presence, I leave worms and moles alone, for you cannot have one without the other.

Mice and voles, on occasions, do damage which earns them loss of status and punishment marks. A pair of short-tailed voles last year nipped off at soil level, about 40 cauliflower seedlings over-wintering in a frame. I found the tops in a pile behind a row of pots. How the voles gained access to the frames puzzled me until I found a hole at the back. Now the frame is both vole and mouse-proofed with small-meshed wire netting.

For several years there was always a tawny owl or two in the process of being fostered or healed and mice and voles being in great demand as food, were never a problem or plague. Unfortunately, *Crocus* are looked on as food by certain, ill-intentioned rodents. Possibly if they devoured the corms before those promising, fat orange-yellow shoots pushed up it would seem less of an act of vandalism on their part. Dowsing the soil with an animal repellent, burying twigs of gorse above the bulbs, or laying down fine mesh netting until the flower buds show, are all methods worth trying. Once, in total exasperation at having hundreds of species *Crocus* destroyed, I borrowed a shotgun and two cartridges. The culprit duly presented itself, I let fly with both barrels, and the animal sat up and groomed itself. As if to compensate for their bad habits, bank voles do eat quantities of insects. My neighbour's cat has a hunting range which includes my garden and spends hours patiently pursuing, and let it be said, eating voles. So a vole's life is not all *Crocus* corms and slugs for main course.

For two years I blamed voles for eating peas and broad beans just as they were sprouting. Last year I had to focus my wrath on wood mice when two turned up in my specimen traps set under cloche in a pea row. I find that placing pieces of carrot and apple tempt them away from the peas. And watering down the rows with a repellent after sowing, then putting a cloche over the bed, stops all damage.

Remember that not all mouse-like creatures are pests; shrews, for example, eat insects and should therefore be cherished!

Moles I am learning to live with: they appear to do little harm.

Specific problems – the snake in your Eden!

Bullfinches do enormous harm in some years to the buds on certain trees. I remember one year when every single bud except those at the tips of every slender twig were stripped from an avenue of flowering cherries in my last garden. Here, it is usually the damson which suffers along with several ornamental, flowering shrubs. Spraying with bird deterrents, placing an imitation hawk near threatened trees, even covering smaller shrubs with netting are all worth trying. Fortunately, damage has declined here in recent years, due perhaps, to the activities of a sparrowhawk which occasionally makes sweeps over the garden.

Grey squirrels are a most persistent aggravation which I view very much as a foreign intruder, unlike our beautiful red squirrel. In forests grey squirrels are trapped, shot, and generally harassed, which makes a garden stocked regularly with food a sanctuary and never failing squirrel larder. So in a garden where living is easy and persecution non-existent, grey squirrels can quickly become pests. There is a humane trap recommended by the Forestry Commission which catches and holds the victim unharmed. The problem then is what to do with an extremely angry, active grey squirrel once it is caught. There is a solution which immediately suggests itself, but I suspect it would be against the law. Take the unwilling captive into the nearest park or woodland and then release it. Somewhere in the same class of anti-social behaviour as throwing weeds over the neighbour's fence. Grey squirrels are vermin, so calling in the local pest control officer is a facility those living in built up areas might take advantage of. There is no way I have tried other than trapping or shooting which will deter them: they are, like the brown rat, an introduced pest and almost as hard to control.

Fortunately, 'no-go' areas can be contrived. I hang nut dispensers on wires threaded through a piece of shiny, slippery metal – tin hammered flat will do very well providing the edges are blunted and made safe. Drilling holes in the bottom of a bottle and then threading the wire through with the dispenser above it is a method adopted by a friend. Bird-tables are especially vulnerable to such an agile animal. The RSPB suggests covering the post with a section of plastic drain pipe, cut to length so it reaches to within six inches (15 cm) of the table level. Then cut a hole in a biscuit tin and slip it over the top of the post, upside down, so it rests on the top of the plastic drain pipe. The entertainment value of this device amply repays the time spent in construction. Squirrels shin up the plastic pipe quite effortlessly, then in trying to scramble over the tin lose their grip and slide back to the ground. I am only sorry that as yet no one has succeeded in translating what the frustrated squirrel is saying after the fifteenth attempt. My method is simply to put two strips of the grease band used to protect fruit trees against winter moth, around the post, spaced just a squirrel's reach apart. They hate the tacky surface and do not cross.

All nestboxes should have a metal protector fitted to stop squirrels, woodpeckers, and other ill-intentioned intruders enlarging the hole. The lid should also be securely fastened down; squirrels soon learn the trick of removing an unlatched flap.

There are other unwelcome visitors to the bird table which are less easily kept away, although what may be defined as undesirable in

R H Fisher

Badgers are rare garden visitors, but may have a track that they use regularly.

one area might be happily acceptable in another. Gulls are an example of the opportune guzzler, particularly in coastal gardens. Starlings and sparrows are also thought by some to be not strictly 'U'. I happen to like both, especially starlings, whose ability to mimic almost any other bird call is quite remarkable. To hear a cock turkey gobbling from a chimney pot, or a curlew calling from the ash tree only to discover the perpetrator to be a starling, makes this bird special. The star performer for me was the bird which could reproduce exactly the whistle I used to call my dog. Eventually, the dog became so frustrated she would only answer when called by name. So in spite of feeding a whole bevy of pheasants, most of the inhabitants of a nearby rookery, together with starlings, sparrows and other avian free-loaders all get hungry, just like me. Truth be told, I can think of no way that I could keep starlings out without banning blackbirds also.

Pigeons I have not had to contend with, except in a pie decently covered with a delicately flaking crust, in which case they were more than welcome. I can offer no solution except this one where pigeons are a problem.

There are those who find house martins a nuisance, and I must admit that their ideas of what constitutes a hair tonic dressing can be disconcerting. The simplest, though not easily executed solution, is to place a dropping board below the nest to protect the most vulnerable places, or wear a hat! The twittering of house martins nesting under the eaves and their sometimes raucous conversation on the porch roof below are, through sleep-dulled ears, reminiscent of childhood summer memories.

Rabbits and hares should be prevented from ring-barking trees, especially during very hard weather. One of the best ways is to slip a purpose-made plastic guard around the main stem which is so designed that it expands as growth proceeds. Fencing the entire garden is so prohibitively expensive that it almost necessitates taking out a second mortgage: and your local slug-slurping hedgehog will be barred from entry.

Birds often suffer serious damage when they accidentally fly into windows. The solution is to make the glass visible by either sticking something on it – a string of cut out ducks, or just one or two coloured paper strips as a warning to watch this illusion of space. Fine mesh curtain in strips one inch wide stop little light, do not spoil the picture window effect, yet still effectively warn the birds. To me, windows are for climbing plants like *Rhodochiton*, *Lapageria*, and other thin-stemmed lovelies that marry house and garden together, and are better than a red warning light to the birds.

Other hazards I have suffered and survived include horses with giraffe-like necks eating all they can reach, Highland cattle, five goats which belonged to me anyway, bantam hens which owned me only at feeding time, and a strawberry-eating tortoise. I forgave roe deer, so daintily expressive of wilderness, for eating a whole bed of roses: and a badger family which walked through a wire fence as if it was not there. All play their part in a mini-Eden after the apple eating disaster.

The Joy of Wildlife Gardening

Specially protected wild plants

Adder's-tongue spearwort
Alpine catchfly
Alpine gentian
Alpine sow-thistle
Alpine woodsia
Bedstraw broomrape
Blue heath
Brown galingale
Cheddar pink
Childling pink
Diapensia
Dickie's bladder-fern
Downy woundwort
Drooping saxifrage
Early spider-orchid
Fen orchid
Fen violet
Field cow-wheat
Field eryngo
Field wormwood
Ghost orchid
Greater yellow-rattle
Jersey cudweed
Killarney fern
Lady's-slipper
Late spider-orchid
Least lettuce
Limestone woundwort
Lizard orchid
Military orchid
Monkey orchid
Norwegian sandwort
Oblong woodsia
Oxtongue broomrape
Perennial knawel
Plymouth pear
Purple spurge
Red helleborine
Ribbon-leaved water-plantain
Rock cinquefoil
Rock sea-lavender (two rare species)
Rough marsh-mallow
Round-headed leek
Sea knotgrass
Sickle-leaved hare's-ear
Small Alison
Small hare's-ear
Snowdon lily
Spiked speedwell
Spring gentian
Starfruit

Starved wood-sedge
Teesdale sandwort
Thistle broomrape
Triangular club-rush
Tufted saxifrage
Water germander
Whorled Solomon's-seal
Wild cotoneaster
Wild gladiolus
Wood calamint

Plants and the Law

Unless you have a licence, you may not:

- intentionally pick, uproot or destroy any of the wild plants listed, or even collect their flowers and seeds;
- sell these plants or their seeds if taken from the wild;
- uproot **any** wild plant intentionally, except on your own land or with permission *(the law regarding statement a, page 3).*

As with wild birds and other animals, there are exceptions for the incidental results of lawful operations.

It is not illegal to pick most wild flowers or fruit (such as blackberries), but you should always leave enough to seed and for others to enjoy. We ask you not to pick any wild flowers in a nature reserve. (There may be byelaws which make this illegal anyway.)

Many nurseries and garden centres now sell wild flower seeds and these are to be welcomed for garden use. But as many are of non-British origin they should not be sown 'in the wild' because the mixture of strains could affect our native flora.

(Reproduced from NCC leaflet *Wildlife, The Law and You* (1972) published by the Nature Conservancy Council)

References and other useful books

Aichele, Dietmar. *A Field Guide to Wild Flowers,* Collins

Andrews, Jonathan. *Creating a Wild Flower Garden,* Webb & Bower/Michael Joseph

Baines, Chris. *How to Make a Wildlife Garden,* Elm Tree Books

Boyle, C. L. *RSPCA Book of British Mammals,* RSPCA

Carter, D. *Butterflies and Moths in Britain & Europe,* Pan

Chinery, Michael. *A Field Guide to the Insects of Britain and N Europe,* Collins
  The Natural History of the Garden, Collins

Darlington, Arnold. *Plant Galls in Colour,* Blandford Press

Gibbons, Bob and Liz. *Creating a Wildlife Garden,* Hamlyn

Glue, D. *The Garden Bird Book,* Macmillan

Hamilton, Geoff. *Successful Organic Gardening,* Dorling Kindersley

Hayman, Peter. *Birdwatcher's Pocket Guide,* RSPB/Mitchell Beazley

Hayman, P. and Everett, M. *What's that Bird?* RSPB

Hillier, M. *Manual of Trees & Shrubs,* Hillier Nurseries

Hollom, P. A. D. *The Popular Handbook of British Birds,* H. F. & G. Witherby Ltd

Jones, Derek. *Gardening Wildlife,* Ebury Press

McClintock, D. and Fitter, R. S. R. *Collins Pocket Guide to Wild Flowers,* Collins

Muir, Richard and Nina. *Hedgerows – their History & Wildlife,* Michael Joseph

Phillips, R. *Trees in Britain,* Pan
  Wild Flowers of Britain, Pan

Readers Digest. *Animals of Britain*
  Britain's Wildlife Plants and Flowers

Royal Society for the Protection of Birds. *Gardening with Wildlife*

Stebbings, Bob. *Bats,* Anthony Nelson

Stevens, John. *The National Trust Book of Wild Flower Gardening,* Dorling Kindersley

Stevenson, Violet. *The Wild Garden,* Windward

Thomas, J. A. *Butterflies of the British Isles,* Royal Society for Nature Conservation

Thomas, G. S. *Perennial Garden Plants,* J. M. Dent

Wood, N. *Birds in your Garden,* Hamlyn

Young, Geoffrey. *The Sunday Times Countryside Companion,* Country Life Books

Useful addresses

British Butterfly Conservation Society
Tudor House,
Quorn,
Loughborough, Leicestershire LE12 8AD

British Hedgehog Preservation Society
Knowbury House,
Knowbury,
Ludlow,
Shropshire

British Trust for Conservation Volunteers (BTCV)
London Office: 80 York Way,
London N1 9AG
Head Office: 36 St Mary's Street,
Wallingford,
Oxfordshire OX10 0EH

British Trust for Ornithology (BTO)
Beech Grove,
Tring,
Hertfordshire HP23 5NR

The Cottage Garden Society
c/o Mrs Philippa Carr,
15 Faenol Avenue,
Abergele,
Clwyd LL22 7HT

Fauna and Flora Preservation Society (FFPS)
79-83 North Street,
Brighton,
E Sussex BN1 12A

Field Studies Council
Preston Montford,
Montford Bridge,
Shrewsbury SY4 1HW

Friends of the Earth (FOE)
26-28 Underwood Street,
London N1 7JQ

Greenpeace
30/31 Islington Green,
London N1 8XE

Henry Doubleday Research Association
Ryton Gardens,
Ryton-on-Dunsmor,
Coventry

Nature Conservancy Council (NCC)
Northminster House,
Peterborough PE1 1UA

Royal Horticultural Society
Vincent Square,
London SW1P 2PE

Royal Society for Nature Conservation (RSNC)
The Green,
Nettleham,
Lincoln LN2 2NR

Royal Society for the Protection of Birds (RSPB)
The Lodge,
Sandy,
Bedfordshire SG19 2DL

WATCH
22 The Green,
Nettleham,
Lincoln LN2 2NR

Young Ornithologists' Club (YOC)
The Lodge,
Sandy,
Bedfordshire SG19 2DL

Nurseries

Native plants and seeds

Blooms Nurseries of Bressingham,
Diss,
Norfolk

John Chambers *(seeds, plants)*
15 Westleigh Road,
Barton Seagrave,
Kettering,
Northamptonshire NN15 5AJ

Emorsgate Seeds *(seeds)*
Emorsgate,
Terrington St Clement,
King's Lynn,
Norfolk PE34 4NY

Kingsfield Tree Nursery *(plants, trees and shrubs)*
Winsham,
Chard,
Somerset TA20 4JF

Landlife Wild Flowers Ltd (RPA) *(seeds, plants)*
The Old Police Station,
Lark Lane,
Liverpool L17 8UU

Nordybank Nurseries *(seeds, plants)*
Clee St Margaret,
Craven Arms,
Shropshire SY7 9EF

Poyntzfield Herb Nursery *(plants, medicinal)*
Black Isle,
By Dingwall,
Ross and Cromarty IV7 8LX

The Seed Bank *(seeds, seed exchange)*
Cowcombe Farm Herbs,
Gipsy Lane,
Chalford,
Stroud,
Gloucestershire GL6 8HP

Stoke Lacy Herb Garden,
Bromyard,
Herefordshire HR7 4JH

Suffolk Herbs *(seeds, plants)*
Sawyers Farm,
Little Cornard,
Sudbury,
Suffolk CO10 0NY

Ponds and water gardens

Stapeley Water Gardens Ltd
Stapeley,
Nantwich,
Cheshire CW5 7LH

Maydencroft Aquatic Nurseries
Maydencroft Lane,
Gosmore,
Hitchin,
Hertfordshire

G. Mimack
The Water Plant Farm,
Woodholme Nursery,
Stock,
Essex

Wildwoods Water Garden Centre
Theobalds Park Road,
Crews Hill,
Enfield,
Middlesex EN2 9BP

Index

Index

Index